Janis Just

Jihad 2.0

The Impact of Social Media on the Salafist Scene and the Nature of Terrorism

Anchor Academic Publishing

Just, Janis: Jihad 2.0: The Impact of Social Media on the Salafist Scene and the Nature of Terrorism, Hamburg, Anchor Academic Publishing 2015

Buch-ISBN: 978-3-95489-338-6
PDF-eBook-ISBN: 978-3-95489-838-1
Druck/Herstellung: Anchor Academic Publishing, Hamburg, 2015
Covermotiv: fotolia.com, © Oleg_Zabielin
Covergestaltung: Rieke Heinze

Bibliografische Information der Deutschen Nationalbibliothek:
Die Deutsche Nationalbibliothek verzeichnet diese Publikation in der Deutschen Nationalbibliografie; detaillierte bibliografische Daten sind im Internet über http://dnb.d-nb.de abrufbar.

Bibliographical Information of the German National Library:
The German National Library lists this publication in the German National Bibliography. Detailed bibliographic data can be found at: http://dnb.d-nb.de

All rights reserved. This publication may not be reproduced, stored in a retrieval system or transmitted, in any form or by any means, electronic, mechanical, photocopying, recording or otherwise, without the prior permission of the publishers.

Das Werk einschließlich aller seiner Teile ist urheberrechtlich geschützt. Jede Verwertung außerhalb der Grenzen des Urheberrechtsgesetzes ist ohne Zustimmung des Verlages unzulässig und strafbar. Dies gilt insbesondere für Vervielfältigungen, Übersetzungen, Mikroverfilmungen und die Einspeicherung und Bearbeitung in elektronischen Systemen.

Die Wiedergabe von Gebrauchsnamen, Handelsnamen, Warenbezeichnungen usw. in diesem Werk berechtigt auch ohne besondere Kennzeichnung nicht zu der Annahme, dass solche Namen im Sinne der Warenzeichen- und Markenschutz-Gesetzgebung als frei zu betrachten wären und daher von jedermann benutzt werden dürften.

Die Informationen in diesem Werk wurden mit Sorgfalt erarbeitet. Dennoch können Fehler nicht vollständig ausgeschlossen werden und die Diplomica Verlag GmbH, die Autoren oder Übersetzer übernehmen keine juristische Verantwortung oder irgendeine Haftung für evtl. verbliebene fehlerhafte Angaben und deren Folgen.

Alle Rechte vorbehalten

© Anchor Academic Publishing, Imprint der Diplomica Verlag GmbH
Hermannstal 119k, 22119 Hamburg
http://www.diplomica-verlag.de, Hamburg 2015
Printed in Germany

Table of content

1. Introduction 7
2. Ideology of Islamism and global Jihad 13
3. The ideology of political Islam and the West 17
    3.1 Samuel Huntington's "clash of civilizations"-theory 18
    3.2 Competing values 21
    3.3 Globalization and anti-Americanism 23
4. The changing nature of terrorism– Jihadist innovations 25
5. Internet as a motor of change 29
6. Social media networks and the individualization of Jihad 34
    6.1 Jihadism and the media – a short history 35
    6.2 The transformative potential of social media 37
    6.3 The global ummah: From virtual to real-world terrorism 40
    6.4 Forums & Facebook 43
7. Social media strategies of the German Salafi sect 48
    7.1 Salafism in Germany 49
    7.2 The Salafi use of social media 50
        7.2.1. Global Islamic Media Front 51
        7.2.2 Die Wahre Religion – The true religion 54
8. Modern Jihadist characters and the influence of the Internet on the Salafist scene 56
    8.1 Loners, Lone Wolves, Lone Wolf Pack and Lone Attackers 56
    8.2 Al-Qaeda´s magazine and the recruitment of "self-made" Jihadists 58
9. Conclusion 62
10. References 65

1. Introduction

Twelve years after September 11, 2001, the terrorist attacks and the U.S. response – known as the global war on terrorism – have changed the world. Since, terror attacks committed by Jihadist activists are world-wide on the rise concomitantly with acceleration of social, economic and cultural changes and the weakening of political authorities in parts of the world. The arena of terror has become transnational. In the contemporary political climate, religious fundamentalism, ethnic nationalism and in general an anti-Western attitude has provided ideological solutions to the perceived injustice of Western liberalism, secular politics and modernization. Here, modernization implies more than just a replacement of the old by the new: "It implies a shift from a society in which people's social and legal status is largely determined by characteristics they are usually born with, such as sex, religion and family, to one in which social and legal status is largely determined by what people achieve by their own effort." (Munson 1988, p. 108-109)

Militant Islamism with its transnationally planned, organized and executed attacks has become a global ideology in terms of a body of ideas upon which particular political, economic, or social systems and movements developed. Since the attacks that are commonly referred to as 9/11, defeating the global Jihadist movement (GJM) – which defines in this book the universe of Jihadist groups that are associated with or inspired by al-Qaeda – remains the most pressing security challenge facing the United States, but also Europe, Asia and Africa. Compared to traditional or regional Jihadist groups, which aim against local adversaries with usually limited goals and a limited geographic scope, the global Jihadist movement targets its foes across the globe and pursues broad geopolitical aims. At its core, the ideology of the GJM is profoundly transnational in the sense that it attempts to contextualize local conflicts as part of a broader struggle against "infidels", "apostates" and a secular culture. Its political theology has been described by many scholars as a sort of religious Fascism. It is supremacist, idealizes the historic stage of the dawn of Islam; "re-actualizes" historic collective myths; it is totalitarian in essence; rejects liberal democracy, glorifies war and death, emphasizes the collective over the individual and strives to re-engineer a period of the ancient period.

Salafism is a branch of radical Islam based in Saudi Arabia that seeks to establish an Islamic empire (Caliphate) across the Middle East, North Africa and Europe – and eventually the entire world. Although Salafists make up only a fraction of the estimated 4.3 million Muslims in Germany, authorities are concerned that most of those attracted to Salafi ideology are impressionable young Muslims who are especially susceptible to committing terror attacks in the name of Islam. This work focuses on the militant wing, on those who are eager in supporting or exercising militant operations.

The information revolution and the exponential rise of the Internet is a global phenomenon which, alongside other manifestations of globalization and late modernity, will likely come to define our period of human history as enlightenment or industrial revolution has previous centuries. The fact that the Internet has revolutionized our lives has become a truism to say. Yet, the world-wide web has transformed the way we communicate. It has transformed the way people talk, write, shop, socialize; it has reduced the costs of communication and opened an easy access to the world's knowledge. Beyond national borders and across great distances, it has made it easier to find like-minded people and create new social networks of interest. It offers a way of communication where users can act anonymously and from all around the globe. Apart from remote regions of Africa and Asia, Internet penetration is not limited to particular demographics or social class.

After the Islamist motivated murder of a British Army soldier in London on May 22, 2013, the perpetrators encouraged witnesses to take out their phones and videotape their statement. Margaret Thatcher pronounced in 1985 that "publicity is the oxygen of terrorism". Today, it is not the TV broadcaster that decides what is being broadcasted throughout the world, but the terrorists determine themselves whether to embrace the media as a tool to gain attention, inspire fear or recruit new members. That is why terrorists of any background have adopted the Internet as one of their tools of trade. Jihadists have managed to retain control of the narrative and maintain ideological coherence to a large degree.

Terrorists can use the Internet for a wide range of purposes; Islamist extremists are increasingly adopting the Internet as an instrument for reconnaissance, training, coordination and fund raising. The rise of instant-messaging, blogging, video sharing, and social-networking platforms have made it more difficult to remove or restrict particular types of content in practical terms. Rather than static websites, which serve only one purpose at a time and may be filtered, the interactive platforms that carry much of today's online traffic have hundreds of millions of users uploading, posting, and re-posting terabytes of data every minute. Furthermore, the majority of violent extremist content is now embedded in privately owned platforms as for example YouTube or Facebook. The new threat of cybercrime and cyber-terrorism has been a matter of debate in recent years[1] and brought up a special branch within intelligence services around the world. However, this paper does not try to explore this operational use of the Internet but will focus on its communicative functions as a tool to spread propaganda, information and mobilize potential supporters. The study at hand aims to explore the ardent enthusiasm of Islamist extremists to exploit communicative innovations in order to reach larger audiences quickly, cheaply and anonymously. I shall argue that progressive technology and the modern Internet landscapes have created new types of social arena and helped Islamist radicals to cultivate the networks, relationships and bonds that prerequisite to violent radicalization and terrorism. These changes modified the organizational structures of the GJM and lead to an emergence of new types of Jihadi terrorists.

In this book, the primary intention is to cast a preliminary analytical eye onto the troublesome new development of Jihadist action within the broader context of radical Islam. The objective of this book is neither an analysis of the strategy or structure of the GJM or al-Qaeda nor is it an interpretation of Internet history. But it should deliver an understanding of how the emergent online environment has been influencing and globalizing a religiously fundamental movement that actually rejects ideas of enlightenment and modernity. An analysis of any radicalization process cannot be separated from an analysis of the social environment in which the individual had been socialized. Especially regarding new forms of terrorism like the

---

[1] See i.e. the yearly reports of the Bundeskriminalamt (Federal Criminal Police Office) on http://www.bka.de/nn_193360/DE/Publikationen/JahresberichteUndLagebilder/Cybercrime/cybercrime__node.html?__nnn=true

Islamist one, a social-psychological approach[2] and an analysis of its ideology is substantial in understanding the phenomenon of global Jihad.

The practical research which serves as a supplement and support for the theoretical discourse analysis was carried out over a period of four months between January and April 2013. This qualitative approach was conducted with a fictive German character on the social media platform Facebook. The character pretends to be a male German Muslim convert in his mid-30´s and had a Facebook history of two years in which he was continuously making online friendships and getting acquainted with followers, leaders and groups of the German and international Salafist movement. The character has engaged in the different networks as an observer and entered frequently into a dialogue through comments, "likes", and own postings concerning Islamic religious and political issues. This research does not constitute a representative sample but has proven to be useful in underpinning arguments and finding current examples. In my case, the methodological approach does not serve to create a new theory, but rather uses existing theories and concepts to facilitate the research on the given phenomena aiming to inform the reader on the trends, the background and context in which the object of research, Islamist fundamentalism, has grown.

In order to study Salafi Jihadism, whether on the Internet or offline, it is necessary to define what constitutes the Salafist ideology. In *chapter 2*, I follow up on the history of Jihadism and consider the question whether Jihadism is a revolutionary act against oppression. In times of ubiquitous identity crises, the Salafi law and order version of Islam provides meaning and security especially to those individuals who feel disadvantaged and excluded from society. The Salafi counter culture is not only attracting young Muslims with migration backgrounds in the second or third generation but young Germans who are looking for a strong community as well.

Discussions about "civilization" and current political ideologies and cultures will necessarily lead to the theses of Samuel Huntington. Chapter 3 aims to introduce into the debate triggered by Samuel Huntington and Francis Fukuyama with the

---

[2] A profound analysis of the individual psychology of suicide terrorism that is firmly established in Jihadist ideology to gain special recognition as a "martyr" is presented by Schmidtbauer, Wolfgang (2003): *Der Mensch als Bombe. Eine Psychologie des neuen Terrorismus.* Hamburg: Rowohlt.

leading question of how the world changed after the fall of the Berlin wall and the Soviet empire. The battle of ideologies is in their focus, while Huntington's "clashing civilizations" are perhaps best illustrated by the renewed conflict between radical Islam and the West. Much of the Islamic world perceives an assault on the religion of Mohammed by Western culture, led by the United States, Israel and Europe. *Chapter 3* connects the preceding broader background with an analysis of essential parts in Salafist ideology, be it the anti-Western sentiment or the critical stance towards modern globalization. Also known as Wahhabis, Salafists believe – among other anti-Western doctrines – that democracy must be destroyed and replaced with an Islamic form of government.

Terrorism is the active constituent of Jihadism and the popular means for the GJM. *Chapter 4* describes the transition of old terrorism into its new form and provides a definition for one of the most contested terms in Social and Political sciences. The ideological goals of modern, Jihadist terrorists have shifted from surgical and symbolic acts towards indiscriminate attacks against random civilians that are inferior "infidels" in the eyes of the perpetrators.

After this analysis of both, the ideological and practical components of Jihadist beliefs, the paper continues with a theoretical background of the Internet as a motor of change in the globalized world. *Chapter 5* will be looking at different schools of thoughts regarding the potential of new media. The question of education and mediation of ideology through the Internet as well as its possible impact on society and democratization will be considered.

Chapter 6 examines the newly promoted Salafist strategy of individualization in the Jihadist struggle with the means of social media. As part of this trend, the supporters of the GJM are using Facebook, one of the largest, most popular and diverse social networking sites, both in the United States and globally, to propagate operational information in multiple languages. Some tactical information is available on Facebook, but the majority of Salafist use of Facebook focuses on disseminating ideological information and exploiting the site as an alternative media outlet for their propaganda and recruitment. While social networking sites have recently become popular with radicals, forums have long been used by terrorists to exchange ideas, and spread ideological, tactical and operational information among a sympathetic audience.

Chapter 7 presents the German Salafist scene and exemplarily studies their use of social media sites. In recent years, Germany has brought up a new generation of so-called "homegrown" Jihadists who are born in Germany and either converted to Islam and radicalized or radicalized their domestic Muslim faith. Salafism is the fundamentalist interpretation of the Islamic Holy Scriptures. The adherents of this radical Islamic version aspire to involve in modern communication and lead debates on social media platforms in order to spread their indoctrination and to recruit new companions. The "Global Islamic Media Front" and the Salafist group named "Die Wahre Religion" (Engl.: The true religion) are two examples of this endeavor spearheading the German Salafist scene each of them with their own interpretation of Jihadist struggle.

The GJM has not only changed the traditional nature of terrorism but it has also mastered the art of transforming initial conspiracy group structures into a social movement. Since 9/11, the US-lead "war on terror" has brought great losses especially under the leading figures of the GJM and domestic intelligence services and authorities are aware of the Salafist threat. *Chapter 8* reviews the many changes of the global Jihad movement in their strategies and within the process of radicalization. Under the umbrella of a collective ideology, individuals can connect via the Internet and radicalize without a necessity for personal face-to-face contact. Within this phenomenon of autodidactic Jihad, self-made cells of "Lone-Wolf"-Jihadists emerge preparing for a terrorist incident without any connection to hierarchically organized military groups. Lone-wolves are driven by the global ideology of Jihad and are instructed by material published in forums, social media platforms or magazines available on the Internet. With their English language magazine "Inspire", al-Qaida is eagerly supporting this trend that adapts the new needs of the movement. Al-Qaida gives technical details for possible plots and urges Muslims living in Western countries of target, to carry out attacks by themselves or in small autonomous groups.

2. Ideology of Islamism and global Jihad

Islamist[3] militancy has risen significantly in the last decade, with many European countries reporting a steep rise in the number of individuals classified as "potential violent extremists". Not all Islamists are terrorists, but the framework of Islamism as an ideological bedrock can be regarded as an incubator for militant operations under the flag of Jihadist Islam.

This paper frequently uses the terms "Islamism", "Salafism" and "Jihadism". It has been written in some detail about the history of labels for Islamic movements respectively their protagonists and the semantic differences[4]. However, the term "Jihadism" needs some clarification as it has often been labeled a clumsy and controversial term in readings and discussions. Especially because "Jihad" is an important religious term of Islam and can refer to an individual spiritual motive of living according to Islamic laws. It can also refer to the act of defending Islam with violent methods. The concrete word "Jihadism" is a neologism and therefore not native to Islamic history. As stated by Jerret Brachman (2009, p. 5), the term has been employed out of convenience because it "communicates a vital point: namely, that al-Qaeda and groups like it are distinguished from other Muslims by their singular focus on the violent side of the Jihad concept. In recent years, the 'Jihadism' label has been validated as the least worst option across the Arab-speaking world, appearing throughout Arab television and print media." The world's counter-terrorism community almost commonly uses that term to refer to Muslims who use violence in order to pursue their universalistic political agendas.

---

[3] In most newspaper articles and academic literature there is a reluctance to identify acts of terrorism with the teachings of one of the world's great religions or to recognize the derivation of the jihad phenomenon from the tenets of Islam. Whether the simple use of terms like "Islamic terrorism" is a discrimination of a whole religion or whether it could actually be regarded as a precise and profound description of a modern phenomenon that is taking its ideology from nothing less than the foundation of a fundamentally political religion, the Quran, is a discourse too controversial to be examined only briefly.

[4] See i.e.: Martin Kramer (2003): *Coming to Terms: Fundamentalists or Islamists?* In: Middle East Quarterly, Spring 2003 Vol.2, 65-77 and Cook, David (2005): *Understanding Jihad.* California: University Press

> „The jihadist ideology combines the extreme and minority interpretation [jihadi-Salafi] of Islam with an activist-like commitment or responsibility to solve global political grievances through violence. Ultimately, the jihadist envisions a world in which jihadi-Salafi Islam is dominant and is the basis of government." (NYPD 2007, p. 8)

Any equation of terrorism with acts of revolution as a response to a repressive state needs to be treated with great caution. In his review of the psychological causes of terrorism, Moghaddam (2005) states that "material factors such as poverty and lack of education are problematic as explanations of terrorist acts" (p. 162). It would be an over-simplification to propose that deprivation and oppression provoke acts of terrorism or the membership in one of the Jihadist groups. Moghaddam is not alone with his argument that a mere economic explanation can be neglected. A reduction in poverty or an increase in educational attainment would not seem to have an effect on the reduction of Jihadist terrorism as Krueger and Maleckova demonstrate in their analysis that leads both to the conclusion that "(...) any connection between poverty, education and terrorism is indirect, complicated and probably weak." (Krueger, Alan B.; Maleckova, Jitka 2003, p. 1).

Marc Sageman (2006) argues in the same direction and points out that most of the global Salafi terrorists have some occupational skills and were often studying or working in the technical fields, such as engineering, architecture, or computers: "In terms of extent of education, about 60 percent of global Salafi terrorists had some form of college education in contrast with their peers from their respective countries where higher education is relatively rare." (p. 126) Surprisingly, he states, that very few of those terrorists were formally educated in religion: "[P]aradoxically, the future terrorists were very well educated, but lacked any religious education. It was (...) this combination of technical education and lack of religious sophistication that made them vulnerable to an extreme interpretation of Islam." (p. 127)

Although any comprehensive future vision of Jihadist goals is hardly to be found there are recurring pronouncements emphasizing certain themes and a selective interpretation of Islamic law and history. In the common historical perception of Jihadists

> "[t]here is a war of civilization in which 'Jews and Crusaders' are seeking to destroy Islam; armed jihad is the individual obligation of every Muslim; terrorism and other asymmetric strategies are appropriate for defeating even the strongest powers, Islam is under siege by Christians, Jews, secularists, and globalization; and the economy of the United States is its vulnerable 'center of gravity'." (Rabasa et al 2006, p. xviii)

According to Reuven Paz (2010, xxxvii), "the new ideology took on the dimensions of a global terrorist struggle, justified by the perception that the jihad, like the Palestinian struggle, was an act of self-defense against a Western-Jewish global conspiracy."

There are many different perspectives and estimations on the roots of global Jihad. Paz (2010, xxxvii) recognizes the beginning of global Jihad in the collaboration of Egyptian and Palestinian Islamic jihad during the late 1970s and early 1980s and in the flow of Arab and Muslim volunteers to Afghanistan in the 1980s and to Bosnia, Albania, Kosovo and Chechnya during the 1990s. The massive terrorism against Israel over the past three decades contributed as well. Hanna Rogan (2006, p. 8) dates back modern militant Islamism to the 1930`s[5] whereas global Jihadism appeared as a relatively new phenomenon in the mid 1990´s when Osama bin-Laden declared the West to be the greatest enemy of the Muslim world and urged his followers to fight this enemy, irrespective of territorial boundaries:

> "The focus then shifted from the near enemy (local 'kufr', or infidel, regimes) to the far enemy (the West) and supporters of this global Jihad started carrying out attacks in the West as well as on western interests in the Muslim world. The al-Qaeda organization was the base for global jihadism, and its training camps in Afghanistan provided the supporters with ideological information, paramilitary training, and personal relations." (Rogan 2006, p. 8)

---

[5] For a closer look upon militant Islamism in the 1930´s and the cooperation between the powerful Grand Mufti of Jerusalem and the National Socialists that had been overlooked for many years, Klaus Peter Mallmann & Martin Cüppers (2010) deliver a comprehensive analysis in: *Halbmond und Hakenkreuz. Das 'Dritte Reich', die Araber und Palästina.* Darmstadt: Primus Verlag

Attacking Western targets in a self-defensive manner is a common moral conviction of Sunni jihadists such as al-Qaeda and Hamas although the latter has developed in particular in the context of Palestinian nationalism and resistance to Israel (Croitoru 2007). Beyond this basic analysis and program, Jihadism leaves many issues open:

> "No single state, movement or leader furnishes a model for all of its exponents. Islamists may view Iran or the Taliban regime in Afghanistan in a positive or negative light. They may disagree to the point of fighting among themselves. Sunni and Shi`a Islamists may champion the cause of their denomination and hate the other one or, at times, cooperate. Islamists may or may not favor a leading role for clerics or be led by self-taught figures whose level of theological knowledge is quite low." (Rubin 2010, xix)

Hezbollah is an example of Shi'a Jihadism, but it, too, is more appropriately defined by its Lebanese context and ties to Iran and its ambitions for regional hegemony. Neither they nor Hamas seem largely motivated by the universalistic ambitions of al-Qaeda, but both make similar arguments on behalf of terrorism and suicide bombings. These decided anti-American, ideologically anti-Semitic and anti-Western tenets that regularly leads to attacks in the name of Allah as well as the ensuing US-lead "war on terror" brought a world-wide focus on religious fundamentalism and Islamic culture opposing secular democratic values (Tibi 2002, pp. 166 f.).

3. The ideology of political Islam and the West

As previously indicated the fundamental aspect in the Jihadist radicalization process is ideology. As reported by the New York Police Department (NYPD) in their study about radicalization of Islamist terrorists that had been socialized in the West, "Jihadist or jihadi-Salafi ideology is the driver that motivates young men and women, born or living in the West, to carry out 'autonomous jihad' via acts of terrorism against their host countries. It guides movements, identifies the issues, drives recruitment and is the basis for action." (NYPD 2007, p.6) An example for substantial value differences between the "home-grown" Salafi "counter-culture" (Horst 2012) and Western secularism are "Sharia controlled zones" in some London boroughs established in 2011. Pasted on bus stops and street lamps, posters convey the message that there is to be "no gambling", "no music or concerts", "no porn or prostitution", "no drugs or smoking" and "no alcohol" in the areas the posters are displayed. The Islamic rules are enforced by Islamist street gangs that are physically intervening against contraventions[6]. According to the Islamic information and news site "kavkazcenter.com" (2013, January 23, para. 9), the Islamist activists in London announce their struggle against the Western way of life: "This will mean this is an area where the Muslim community will not tolerate drugs, alcohol, pornography, gambling, usury, free mixing between the sexes - the fruits if you like of Western civilization. We want to run the area as a Sharia-controlled zone and really to put the seeds down for an Islamic Emirate in the long term." With this kind of arguments, the ideologues manage to declare the "Westernized" British society as infidels and therefore legitimate targets of Jihad.

The fall of the Berlin Wall 1989 marked the end of the Cold war era and offered the chance for new paradigms to develop. Two major, yet contrasting views emerged. The first view was advocated by Francis Fukuyama in his article "The End of History?"[7]. In his article, Fukuyama claims that "history", meaning major human conflicts, had come to an end with the collapse of the Soviet Communism. The new world order, he argued, would be immune from significant ideological challenges and future conflicts would be limited to local nuisances that posed no direct threat to

---

6 See: *Muslims enforcing Sharia law on the streets of London* (2013 January 17). Retrieved from http://www.youtube.com/watch?v=E8gA03rXifM&feature=youtu.be on February 2, 2013
7 Fukuyama, Francis: The End of History?, in: The National Interest (1989) 16, 3-18

Western values and Western civilization. The second view was subsequently articulated by Samuel Huntington. The controversial article of the Harvard professor "The Clash of Civilizations?"[8] was published in 1993. He argues that ethnically volatile regions previously held as stable satellite entities by the Cold War powers would gradually erupt and that these associations among culturally alike states are taking the place of traditional Cold War ideological alignments as a means for interstate cooperation and alliance.

3.1 Samuel Huntington's "clash of civilizations"-theory

The debate about civilization inevitably has to mention the contradictory potential between the Islamic and the Western civilization. A part of the problem of taking about civilization hereby lies in the very notion of the term itself. It is an intrinsically positional and evaluative concept, claiming that one side has it and the other does not. Nonetheless civilization is not a single or directional process created through and within society[9], but rather a set of processes in which a dominant group seeks to impose its own standards of behavior, its own practices, prejudices and assumptions about good and bad behavior.

Concerns about civilizational revivalism and conflict were best reflected in the debate primed by Huntington who was trying to give a new model of world order five years after the end of the Cold-War. He published his theses 1993 respectively 1996 in his most argued book "Clash of Civilizations and the Remaking of World Order". His main argument is that people's cultural and religious identities will be the primary source of conflict in the post-Cold War world. He creates a world with around seven different cultural regions which struggle for supremacy. The "major civilizations" include "Western, Confucian, Japanese, Islamic, Hindu, Slavic-Orthodox, Latin American and possibly African civilization." (Huntington 1993, p.

---

[8] Huntington, Samuel P., 1993: The Clash of Civilizations?, in: Foreign Affairs 72 (1993) 3, 22-49
[9] Concepts of the creation of society can derive from different theoretical models. According to Karl Marx, human beings are collective and individual initiators of history and yet have lost control of many of their creations. History is a human product but it has been made in ways that took control out of their own hands: "Men make their own history, but they do not make it just as they please; they do not make it under circumstances chosen by themselves, but under circumstances directly encountered, given and transmitted from the past." (Marx 2008 [1852], p.15). Theodor Adorno and Max Horkheimer (2002, p. 153) point out in their Critical Theory of "Dialectic of Enlightenment": "Civilization is the triumph of society over nature".

25) By these civilizations, Huntington means something similar to cultures, but also something broader and deeper than the way culture is usually conceived. According to Huntington civilizations are families of cultures and have distinctive ways of thinking and living because they share the same basic philosophical heritage. The secular culture of places as Europe or the United States stands in this conceptualization as subsets of Christendom and Western civilization. Similarly there are subsets forming the Islamic civilization with diverse nations as Egypt, Iran, Saudi-Arabia, Pakistan, and Syria. It could be easily understood that to be a nation within one civilization means that it is part of a homogenous conglomerate without disharmony. This surely does not reflect the multifaceted struggles for example between the Shi`ite and Sunni-Islamic countries but can explain a certain supranational ideology of an Islamic spirit. Considering the majority of the non-secular Islamic states and their religious-political ideology "Islam may be able to absorb some liberal references, but, ultimately, it is a vision of submission to God (…) and a certain social order." (Murden 2011, p. 423)

Huntington claims that the "clash of civilizations" will occur on two levels: the micro- and the macro level. At the micro-level different neighboring groups will get into a certain state of conflict along so-called cultural fault lines, fighting over the control of territories. At the macro-level, states with different cultural ties are struggling for military and political influence and domination and for control over international bodies and third parties (Huntington 1993, p. 49). Huntington`s pointed theory has been accused of conceptual as empirical problems and led to many controversies, mainly because he stated an increasing antagonism between the Western and the Islamic civilization due to their universalistic approach (Murden 2011, p. 421). However, regarding the growing influence of Islamist movements, as for example the government takeover of the Muslim Brotherhood in Egypt in 2012, Huntington presents a foundation for further research and discussion. The anti-Western sentiment, as it will be analyzed further below, constitutes an integral ideology of politicized Islam and is strongly prevalent within the Salafi movement.

Historically, the proliferation of the West was driven by the search for new capital opportunities but also by the pursuit of political empire and the thirst for scientific discovery.

> "The scientific revolution had no direct territorial reference at all, but was critical for the expansion of trade and empire. The Western market economy extended to various areas not or only minimally under the political control of the European imperial centres, even though the whole enterprise would have failed without their active support." (Beyer 1994, p. 53)

The Frankfurt School with its notion of a "Dialectic of Enlightenment" has exemplified that the West cannot be regarded as a linear progressive process of history. It has witnessed horrendous negations of liberty, individualism, and reason. The annihilation of the European Jews, industrially organized by the majority of the German population, became a symbol of the negative, destructive potential of civilization. The Nazis cultivated the anti-Enlightenment notion of an organic nation rooted in blood and soil by eliminating the idea of an individual in favor of the collective unity, the ethnic community, or "Volksgemeinschaft". Anti-Semitism, Racism, slavery, violence, world wars, and totalitarian regimes: These are inherent parts when talking about the history of Western civilization. Philippe Nemo (2005, p. 90) calls these "pre-civilizational" regressions "a betrayal on its own tradition". The German philosopher of the Frankfurt School, Max Horkheimer, argues in the same direction already in 1947:

> "In summary, we are the heirs (...) of the Enlightenment and technological progress. To oppose these by regressing to mere primitive stages does not alleviate the permanent crisis they have brought about. On the contrary, such expedients lead from historically reasonable to utterly barbaric forms of social domination. The sole way of assisting nature is to unshackle its seeming opposite, independent thought." (Horkheimer 1947, p. 127)

Anti-Western ideology has become a modern ingredient in different forms of critique. A crucial point of this anti-Western ideology driven by the global Jihad movement marked the destruction of the World Trade Center and part of the Pentagon – in the eyes of the perpetrators two foremost symbols of the West. Brachman argues that

> "[f]or global Jihadists, Western education creates an army of moral relativists and multiculturalists (...) viewing multiculturalism as a way for Western governments to counteract the growth of Islam as a way of life in Europe and North-America. In short, compromise with the West is an impossibility as its entire civilization is based on beliefs, views and actions that look to subvert Islam. The only solution is disavowal, purification and preparation for war." (Brachman 2009, p. 21)

3.2 Competing values

"The terrible terrorist attack that was unleashed on the United States yesterday was not directed against the American administration, nor against its policies in this or that part of the world. It was an attack planned by people who want to destroy a whole system of values, in effect all that the civilization of "the West" respresents – liberty, democracy, economic power, and military capability."
(Editorial of the Israeli newspaper Ha'aretz on September 12, 2001)

The deliberate destruction of the World Trade Center and part of the Pentagon on September 11, 2001, seemed to vindicate Samuel Huntington's prediction of a "clash of civilizations": terrorists who claim to act in the name of Allah and who disdain Western freedoms are now fighting a war against the West.

Regarding a letter carried by Muhammad Atta, one of the perpetrators of September 11, it unveils that the Islamist terrorists had not in mind to attack an individual country since neither the "United States" nor "America" were mentioned in the letter. Instead the actions were directed against a "civilization of disbelievers" or an amorphous, faceless evil (Paz, 2010, xxxviii). This basic understanding of Islam has, according to Paz, become an initiation of sorts for adherents to global jihad: "They tend to adopt norms of behavior that are simple to understand, and these norms in turn create a basis for unity among different groups and individuals, this sidestepping the difficult terrain of ideological and theological interpretation." (Paz, 2010, xxxviii)

Culture may not be the only major influence on human behavior, but it is certainly one of them. The problem with cultural analysis is that the concept is fiercely and often emotionally embattled. One principal criticism of cultural analysis is that it fails to show how culture works or how cultural identity really affects particular human behavior, especially when it comes to the level of world politics. Reproaching Huntington's argument it has been said that this discourse stood for a political agenda to maintain existing patterns of community, culture and exclusion (Murden 2011, p. 417). Some criticism considered Huntington's downplaying of other factors that influence the behavior of humans and their organizations like the imperatives of economics. Current conflicts are multi-faceted and have political, economic and social dimensions which are playing a very similar role to culture. However, if it comes to Salafi terrorism in particular, that currently constitutes the most violent and aggressive anti-Western movement, a strictly rational explanation about the reasons – especially regarding the trend of suicide attackers – can´t conceive its non-rational dimension. As mentioned above, prevalent attempts of understanding those terrorist incidents bring mostly frustration about economic disadvantages, political repression, or cultural homogenization into effect. But besides those moments, unbridgeable worldview differences[10] need to be taken into account:

> "Osama bin Laden, the Taliban and their Muslim fundamentalist allies (…) see themselves not as individuals with wants and needs, which is a relatively modern notion, but as operatives of Allah. For them, everything is religion, everything faith. In fact, they don't acknowledge any other legitimate way to look at the world. (…) in the madrasas, the Muslim religious schools in Pakistan and Afghanistan, students are strictly forbidden from learning anything except the Koran, (…)The spiritual and the rational can coexist, as they do in almost every society, but Muslim fundamentalist terrorists don't see it that way. (…) their grievance is that their way of thinking is being destroyed by the inundation of Western influences (…).Their mission is to rescue the world from rationality and restore it to religion as they interpret it." (Gabler 2001, para. 3)

The Muslim Brotherhood is one of the Arab´s world most influential social movements. Its original bylaws could be found on the Brotherhood's English language website[11] till 2011 but have since been preserved[12]. These bylaws make clear that the Brotherhood conceives itself as "an international Muslim Body, which seeks to establish Allah's law in the land by achieving the spiritual goals of Islam and the true religion (…) establishing the Islamic State" and "building a new basis of human civilization as is ensured by the overall teachings of Islam (…) The Islamic nation must be fully prepared to fight the tyrants and the enemies of Allah as a prelude to establishing an Islamic state." (IPT 2011, p. 2)

By humiliating the enemies and by making them subhuman Islamist ideology asserts their own moral superiority: "America is called the 'Great Satan' by its enemies in

---

[10] An illustrating phrase willingly used by Islamic radicals i.e.: „You love life, we love death!". See: Küntzel, Matthias (2007): *Jihad and Jew-Hatred*. New York: Press Publishing
[11] www.ikhanweb.com
[12] Screenshot by the Investigative Project on Terrorism (IPT). Retrieved from: http://www.investigativeproject.org/documents/misc/673.pdf, on April 22, 2013.

the Islamic world because, as the predominant Western power, it is both the symbol and the agent of logos. America exports secularism in its popular culture, in its scientific and technological achievements (...)" (Gabler 2001). The United States has been confronted with anti-American or anti-Western aggression in recent years because they so aptly symbolize the notion of secularism, individualism and hedonism (Tibi 2002, pp. 46). These values reject unambiguously the agenda of a religious, abstinent collective as well as a pacifistic notion of a frictionless world collective. The West is being hated for what it stands: individuality, liberalism, an open sexuality; for the opportunity of individual happiness repugnant to the identity of tribe or the self-imposed religious slavery of the "ummah" (Arabic for: the Islamic community). Bassam Tibi states that it were the Islamist extremists who declared – eight years after Huntington's prediction - a war against the West with the ideology of the struggle between Islam and the infidels (Tibi 2002, p. 167).

3.3 Globalization and anti-Americanism

The aforementioned demonization of the United States fits into a process of popular discontent with economic, environmental and political circumstances. Western-style modernism and secularism is often targeted as the enemy, symbolized by Israel and largely by the USA. The slogan of the "American cultural imperialism" symbolizes for many the globalized economy and a blaspheme culture. According to Markovits, anti-Americanism facilitates the substitution of a clear-cut explanation for a more nuanced understanding of the intricate structure of modern societies (Markovits 2004, pp. 118). In a decade where the vast majority of the world population gained access to visual media, to Hollywood movies, soaps and MTV, the images and values that have been projected globally have often been American.

Najjar (2005) argues similarly when he says that for most of those who oppose globalization, it is itself identical with Americanization: "They view globalization as an American design to disseminate American culture as a model for the whole world." Referring to the Jihadist sentiment against the USA and globalization, he states:

> "Radical Islamists view globalization as a new dawa (call) for the elimination of the boundaries between Dar al-Islam (domain of Islam) and

Dar al-Kufr (domain of infidelity). Globalization, they warn, seeks to join the infidels (Western Christians) and Muslims under the banner of secularism and worldliness, leading to unrestricted freedom in the name of human rights, as understood in the West, and to libertinism, the distinguishing characteristics of the decadence of Western civilization. Radical Islamists claim that Islam would resist such calls by 'Crusaders and Jews', in defense of the sharia." (Najjar 2005, p.92)

The anti-American sentiment is not one of peripheral societies only or related to a certain culture. It has its deep roots in European history. Philip Roger (2006) describes the anti-Americanism referring to Michel Foucault as a global discourse with a long past: "Anti-Americanism is an unbridled discourse, not only because it is rife with irrationality and bubbling with humors, but also because it takes an essayistic form, rather than that of a dissertation or a demonstration." (p. xvi) The new wave of globalization in the late twentieth century leads to many novel intercultural interactions and increased markedly the speed at which communities and cultures were changing. The fear of change and the loss of stability is part of an explanation of anti-American sentiments that are hostile towards globalization: "[F]undamentalism often stemmed from a wider fear that existing society was being destroyed. Many fundamentalist groups were born in opposition to the perceived evils of modernity's secularism, pluralism, social atomization, and moral emptiness." (Murden 2011, p. 420) The Salafi Islamic fundamentalism leads to a reversion of collective traditions and Islamic culture. Islamic fundamentalism, in comparison to fundamentalism of other religions, is not just a regional phenomenon but a globalized project that uses modern technology in order to reach their fundamentalist goals: "Despite the visceral antagonism against the social values of modernization, opposition to technological and economic modernization is rare in the fundamentalist Islamic literature." (Munson 1988, p. 108)

4. The changing nature of terrorism– Jihadist innovations

"The Security Council reiterates its concern at the increased use, in a globalized society, by terrorists of new information and communications technologies, in particular the Internet, for the purposes of the recruitment and incitement as well as for the financing, planning and preparation of their activities."
(United Nation`s Security Council, 6765th meeting, May 4, 2012)

The term "terrorism" is perhaps one of the most contentious terms in political science. Literally hundreds of definitions have been coined by scholars and practitioners of politics without any clear consensus on how best to articulate what is unequivocally a significant phenomenon. Defining terrorism is a political challenge as well as an analytical one. This value-laden and pejorative word has a significant role when it comes to analyzing conflict situations. It can be used in order to contrast one side´s legitimate killing to another side´s illegitimate killing.

Some scholars of the liberal left – such as Noam Chomsky or Edward Said –, portray the dominant Western version of terrorism as cynical and hypocritical (Chomsky 2002). They claim that Western states are the worst terrorists. This theory has gained influence in large sections of the global left because of the left´s concern with Third World issues, since colonialism and imperialism seem to offer obvious manifestations of Western state terrorism in action (P. Jenkins 2003, p. 19).

From a methodological perspective, the term terrorism is truly problematic since it can describe a wide array of phenomena. Boaz Ganor (2005), head of the International Institute for Counter-Terrorism, tried to identify the hallmarks of terrorism and its characteristics and proposes the following definition as a starting point for further discussion:

> "Terrorism is a form of violent struggle in which violence is deliberately used against civilians in order to achieve political goals (nationalistic, socioeconomic, ideological, religious, etc.)." (p. 17)

Martin (2011, p. 299) argues that traditional, or old terrorism, was characterized by certain commonalities: "Leftist ethno-nationalist motives; relatively low casualty rates; leftist ideological motives; identifiable organizational profile; surgical and symbolic selection of targets; hierarchical organizational profile; deliberate media manipulation; full-time professional cadres and publicized incidents."

As mentioned earlier, terrorism has many different backgrounds, reasons and purposes. But what is really new on modern forms of Islamist terrorism? Walter Laquer (2000) observes this transformation of traditional terrorism:

> "Traditional terrorism, whether of the separatist or the ideological (left or right) variety, had political and social aims, such as gaining independence, getting rid of foreigners, or establishing a new social order. Such terrorist groups aimed at forcing concessions (…) from their antagonists. The new terrorism is different in character, aiming not at clearly defined political demands but at the destruction of society and the elimination of large sections of the population. In its most extreme form, this new terrorism intends to liquidate all satanic forces, which may include the majority of a country or of mankind, as a precondition for the growth of another, better, and in any case different breed of human. In its maddest, most extreme form it may aim at the destruction of all life on earth, as the ultimate punishment for mankind´s crimes." (p. 81)

Islamist terrorist groups pose different problems for counter-terrorism strategies because they are not interested in money or political gains.

1 Martin 2011, p. 300

	Target Selection	Casualty Rates	Organizational Profile	Tactical / Weapons Selection	Typical Motives
The "old" terrorism	Surgical and symbolic	Low and selective	Hierarchical and identifiable	Conventional and low to medium yield	Leftist and ethnocentric
New terrorism	Indiscriminate and symbolic	High & indiscriminate	Cellular	Unconventional and high yield	Sectarian

Yael Shahar (2005) focuses on the ideological goals when he explicates the "change of motivation" from traditional to modern religiously-driven terrorism:

> "While the traditional terrorist attack was a means to an end – to induce a desired response in the targeted population – the religiously motivated terrorist of the new mode sees the act as an end in itself. The terror attack is meant to bring the war to the enemy, and, in some cases, is seen as a kind of religious act." (p. 78)

The Jihadist terrorists need no longer to worry about alienating prospective supporters, or eliciting a negative press for the organization's cause. Because the cause is sanctioned by God, and thus justifies any means used: "Lacking a rigid political agenda with its concomitant constraints, the modern terrorist is bound only by a unifying religious or apocalyptic ideology." (ibid)

Bruce Hoffman (1997) has pointed out that religious and secular terrorist differ not only in their motivation and goals but also in their constituencies. Secular terrorists "attempt to appeal to a constituency variously composed of actual and potential sympathizers, members of the communities they purport to 'defend', or the aggrieved people they claim to speak for." (p.48) Religious terrorists on the other hand see themselves as being their own constituency: "They execute their terrorist acts for no audience but themselves." (ibid) Main motivation for the single Jihadist is the paradise rather than changing the mundane society. This has serious implications in terms of the acts that such terrorists are willing to carry out: "[T]his absence of a constituency in the secular terrorist sense leads to a sanctioning of almost limitless violence against a virtually opened category of targets – that is, anyone who is not a member of the terrorists' religion or religious sect." (p. 49)

On the basis of the combination of Jihadism, the definition of Jihadist terrorism is as follows according to the National Coordinator for Counterterrorism (2010, p. 78):

> "Jihadist terrorism is terrorism based on jihadist goals. A feature of this category of terrorism is: [Firstly,] [t]he use of the term jihad for the threat of, preparation of, or perpetrating of serious violence against people, or deeds aimed at causing socially-disruptive material damage. [Secondly,] [t]he carrying out of activities which are commensurate with the aim of achieving global dominion of Islam and the re-establishment of the Islamic state."

A much discussed question among scholars on terrorism is why terrorism became such an active constituent within the Islamist scene. For a satisfying answer to this question, a much deeper approach is necessary that would go beyond the scope of this book. Salafi ideology promotes new values, all centered on personal commitment to Islam and the religious community. From this stance a direct need for action ensues, "a new sense of purpose and efficacy born from action." (Sageman 2006, p. 129) Being part of a Salafist or Jihadist group rewards their members with feelings of solidarity within small cliques of like-minded militants: "The terrorism of the global Salafi jihad is grounded in group dynamics under a violent interpretation of Islam, inspiring and guiding the terrorists. Once a participant in this violent social movement, it is difficult for an individual to abandon it without betraying his closest friends (…). The violent global Salafi ideology feeds on this natural and intense loyalty to the group and transforms alienated young Muslims into fanatical terrorists." (ibid, p. 131) According to the Gatestone Institute (2013)[13], more than 1,000 Muslims from across Europe are currently active as Jihadists in Syria, which has replaced Afghanistan, Pakistan and Somalia as the main destination for militant Islamists seeking to obtain immediate combat experience.

Terrorists have traditionally sought to exploit new media to spread their propaganda and to reach potential supporters world-wide with instructions and operational and tactical guidance as it is the case for those volunteers in the Jihad against the Syrian regime. Through websites, forums, blogs, chat rooms etc., Salafists have expanded from a passive use of the Internet into the active creation of websites that create and foster online communities organized around shared affiliations and ideology.

---

[13] Retrieved from http://www.gatestoneinstitute.org/3634/european-jihadists, on April 25, 2013.

5. Internet as a motor of change

Anthony Giddens (2009, p. 724) claims, communication – the transfer of information from one individual or group to the other – to be crucial to any society. Hence, the progression of modern communication systems, from the letter and the telegraph to e-mail and interactive social media is one of great attention. It surely has to be considered as an integral part of any attempt to understand the process globalization. Through the Internet, distance and separation has become more tolerable since it is almost possible to stay in real time-contact while travelling around the world. Giddens (2009, p.728) describes two main scholarly views towards the emergence of the Internet. On the one side there are the scholars who recognize the Internet as a positive addition to human interaction, enhancing and supplementing existing face-to-face relations. Through the ability to meet in free chosen peer groups and the possibility to start a conversation in an anonymous way, new and substantial real-life friendships could result. On the other side there are the more pessimistic scholars who are aware of an increased isolation and atomization created by the time spent interacting in the non-physical world. Giddens summarizes this approach, saying that these scholars

> "(…) argue that one effect of the increasing Internet access in households is that people are spending less 'quality time' with their families and friends. The Internet is encroaching on domestic life as the lines between work and home are blurred: many employees continue to work at home after hours (…). Human contact is reduced, personal relationship suffer, traditional forms of entertainment such as the theatre and books fall by the wayside, and the fabric of social life is weakened." (Giddens, 2009, p.728)

Looking at the recent coup d`états in the Arab world that were often labeled "social media revolutions", there is apparently a revolutionary opportunity in the use of the modern Internet. Social media is an instrument that can – within states with an oppressive regime – be used as a tool to spread the message on an anonymous, cheap and fast way to a large group of people who would support the cause. But at the same time, social media did not develop in an empty space.

For Kevin Kelly (2009, p. 116-121), editor of the US-American "Wired"-magazine, the social media technology offers a new spirit of socialism. He argues that "when masses of people who own the means of production work toward a common goal and share their products in common, when they contribute labor without wages and enjoy the fruits of free charge", it constitutes a "digital socialism". Unlike Bill Gates who once tried to stigmatize open source advocates as a modern sort of communists, Kelly affirms the practical value of this notion of emerging collectivism, like Wikipedia. This modern form of socialism is not "class warfare" and not – as it used to be – an "arm of the state", but rather is "digital socialism", a "socialism without the state. This new brand of socialism currently operates in the realm of culture and economics, rather than government (…)." Most importantly, "it is not an ideology. It demands no rigid creed." (Kelly, 2009, p. 118)

The book of Don Tapscott and Anthony D. Williams with the title "Wikinomics: How Mass Collaboration Changes Everything" argues differently. As one can already interpret by the word "Wikinomics", Tapscott and Williams focus on the economic impact of the "new Internet" and the new mode of production based on collaboration and participation. Laid out as a strategy book for managers and entrepreneurs, it reflects how mass collaboration and the multiple advantages of "digital socialism" can be subsumed under capitalist logic. However, especially the open source movement reflects an order which is to some extend aptly to describe as socialist. This movement which argues for community-developed software is struggling for an open and free access of the source code of programs. The 2001 established project of "BitTorrent", a peer-to-peer file sharing project which allows users to upload their own data libraries and download that of others at the same time, has taken the step in the "great shift from audience to participants (…)." Thomas Friedman (2005, p.95-96) especially appreciates, that this system enables to upload files and globalize the content without going through the traditional hierarchical organizations or institutions: " [Y]ou can now produce really complex things, as an individual or as part of a community, with so much less hierarchy and so much less money than ever before." (Friedman, 2005, p.96) Tapscott and Williams however reproach Friedman as a deputy for open source advocates for his blindness:

> "He sees software, but not the multi-billion dollar ecosystem that surrounds open source. He sees free encyclopedias, but not the rich cultural and educational opportunities that envelope a living, breathing, dynamic repository of knowledge updated by a vast self-organizing community. (…) Friedman is not seeing the forest for the trees."
> (Tapscott/Williams 2006, p.90)

Besides the Internet being handled as a technical source and pool of information, there is the question of education and mediation of ideology through the Internet and the impact on already closed groups and on society as such. What about those who are using the Internet to spread deception, conspiracies and hatred? The new Internet obviously bears not only positive effects. The distribution of conspiracy theories for example could not have grown as strong as it does without the networking power of the Internet.

Jürgen Habermas, practical successor of the Frankfurt School, renewed the liberal thought about the democratic value of the media. In his early work "The Structural Transformation of the Public Sphere" from 1962, Habermas conceives the public sphere as a space where access to information affecting the public good is widely available in his normative model of the media. He aims at a discourse free of domination for all those participating in public debate:

> "Within this public sphere, people collectively determine through rational argument the way in which they wish to see society develop, and this shapes in turn government policy. The media facilitates this process by providing an arena of public debate, and by reconstituting private citizens as a public body in the form of public opinion." (Curran, 2003, p. 233)

In the diversified and modern societies nobody knows everything. The initial function of the creation of a public sphere is therefore one that tries to take into the system the observations and opinions of as many members of society as possible. For Yochai Benkler (2006, p. 198), these members are the potential objects of public concern and consideration. Benkler sees the practices that define the public sphere structured by "an interaction of culture, organization, institutions, economics, and technical communications infrastructure." (Benkler 2006, p. 178)

Referring to Habermas' theory, Anthony Giddens (2009, p. 750) considers two different outcomes of and views on social media platforms. On the one side, he recognizes the revolutionary potential and the pressure Internet-media can build up against authoritarian regimes or "closed" societies. On the other side, the media is increasingly commercializing, influencing the public sphere with different content. "As a result, entertainment will necessarily triumph over controversy and debate, weakening citizen participation in public affairs and shriveling the public sphere."

And Giddens continues pessimistically: "The media, which promised so much, has now become part of the problem with democracy." (Giddens 2009, p. 750)

Barbara Zehnpfennig (2013, pp. 7) argues in a similar direction and illuminates the changes that came with the Internet from the principal of public participation which she regards as a chance and a hazard at the same time. She determines similar to a growing influence of the masses and referring to Alexis de Tocqueville a flipside of the pure public, the impending tyranny of the masses. In her regard, the Internet is a useful tool when used in a dictatorship when it comes to protecting ones rights and lives. In a democracy however, where freedom rights are yet implemented, the Internet can have a contrary effect when "anonymous swarms that are moving through the Internet" are using the medium to distribute opinions without verifiable reason. A superficial super market of opinions has replaced a more balanced exchange of reflected and underpinned arguments. Without education, the Internet provides those without orientation with a wide choice of mostly very simplified information and even disinformation. The Internet as an "unstructured pool of knowledge" cannot replace an understanding of the transported information, news or facts. That leads Zehnpfennig to the conclusion that the Internet is by no means a democratic medium just by itself which is especially interesting after the "Arab Spring"[14] where the Internet was widely glorified as a motor for democratic change. She notes: "Not the Internet leads to democratization but only a handling of it that proceeds with qualitative standards." (Zehnpfenning 2013, p. 7) Transferred to the concerning issue of this book, the Jihadist use of the Internet, this statement by Zehnpfennig can be regarded as a core direction of impact. The Internet is at the nexus of two key trends: the democratization of communications driven by user generated content; and the growing awareness of modern terrorists of the potential of the Internet for their purposes.

---

[14] Even though the common term „Arab Spring" shows a number of 180 million mentions on Google, it can hardly be seen as historically adequate. Not only that it is not correct from a seasonal point of view, it also implies an unwarranted optimism about the outcome that for now brought strictly Islamic groups into power. While the hope of a constructive new democratic spirit in the long-term might be justified, it has been a long and bloody fight for a yet unknown result. A term like "Middle East upheaval" seems rather appropriate. To which degree social media has exactly had its influence on the Arab turmoil 2010/2011 cannot be concluded and it will take some more time before all the forces surrounding these multiple revolutions and uprisings are fully understood. Doubtless, the Internet did serve as a new outlet for expression to disenfranchised populations in Arab countries.

Many benefits of the Internet have been converted to the advantage of groups committed to terrorism. Terrorists require anonymity to exist and to operate in social environments that may not agree with their particular ideology or activities. Decentralized platforms in the Internet provide this anonymity as well as access to communicate from virtually anywhere. Rogan (2006, p. 32) argues that "it is evident that the Internet has transmitted its concept of borderlessness, possible anonymity, and far-reachedness, to jihadism." For Yael Shahar (2005) the network of the GJM is a product of the communications revolution. She even states that "without the Internet al-Qaida would not exist as a global entity. Without the Internet, the Global Jihad would be just the 'Local' Jihad – isolated cells that claim common historical roots." (p.82)

6. Social media networks and the individualization of Jihad

"Without communication, terrorism would not exist."

(Marshall McLuhan, 1978)

The many terrorist attacks against "Western" targets that have taken place across the world since September 11, 2001, from London via Madrid, Bali and Boston to small scale actions and impeded attempts, have clearly other reasons than simply the use of the Internet itself. However, the Internet and especially social media's global reach has offered new ways in which to promote terrorism or Jihad, and thus facilitated its intensification.

The increasing number of public adherents of militant Islamist ideology within the Western hemisphere, local Jihadi forces in African Mali and the drastic radicalization of the Syrian opposition movement in the beginning of the year 2013 are just three very different examples that show how the GJM is outliving the death of one of its most important figureheads, Osama bin Laden. One of the crucial reasons that traditional counter-terrorism measures are presumably failing is that the GJM has changed the traditional nature of terrorism and mastered the art of transforming initial conspirative group structures into a social movement. "Consumers have been transformed into producers" as Brachman (2009, p. 12) claims referring to the Jihadist "social movement" as "a specific type of group action in the fields of sociology and political sciences. It is a large, informal conglomerate of individuals, groups and organizations all focused on making political and social change." For many members of the GJM, al-Qaeda has been regarded as the most important organization in the Salafist struggle because of their successful attempt in calling attention to the self-proclaimed Islamic resistance. The violence in al-Qaeda's action has served to popularize the notion of a radical Islamic resistance in a way never seen before. The next step will likely be one of cultivating a new generation of intellectual, cultural and militant insurgents around the world:

> "By building these organizations, elaborating ideologies, mobilizing constituencies and shaping collective identities, the global Jihadist movement has positioned itself as the catalyst for social change." (Brachman 2009, p.12)

The Internet assists Jihadists in reaching out to a significant audience. It is apparent that online propaganda is spread on a wider basis than traditional written material. Gabriel Weimann (2004) has written extensively on the use of Internet among terrorist groups. He explains why the Internet is such a convenient tool for terrorist networks with its easy access, its fast flow of information, little regulation, and anonymity of communication. Another factor is the potentially huge audience, especially when information available on the Internet is used by the traditional mass media (Weimann 2004, p. 3). Weimann specifies three different audiences targeted by terrorist media groups: Firstly, current and potential supporters, targeted for example with local language sites, items for sale or detailed information about activities. Secondly, there is international public opinion, and in particular foreign journalists, targeted by site versions in different languages: "For the benefit of their international audiences, the sites present basic information about the organization and extensive historical background material (material with which the organization's supporters are presumably already familiar)." (p. 4) Finally, there is the "enemy public". According to Weimann, this audience is not always clearly a target but some sites aim at demonizing the enemy, arousing public debate and changing public opinion in the enemy state (p.5).

6.1 Jihadism and the media – a short history

In his analysis of online Jihadism published for the Washington Institute for Near East Policy in January 2013, Aaron Zelin describes four phases of the Jihadist use of media since 1984. The different periods thereby roughly correspond to the adoption of a new medium for distributing information. In phase one, according to Zelin (2013, p. 4), the Jihadist scene used mainly printed magazines and videotapes with battle scenes and lectures to spread their propaganda. In the mid-1990's and with the growing access to online media, top-down websites held the complete monopoly over what content was important and would be distributed. The websites did not offer spaces for dialogue and interaction, but they still mattered as first ports of call for news, information, and authoritative announcements.

Another milestone was the dissemination of multi-media products, especially video. Until the early 2000's the communication on websites and forums had to be text-based, because Internet bandwidth and people's dial-up connections could not cope with large downloads. When this became possible, audio and later video emerged as powerful drivers of Internet traffic. The propaganda source became less personalized in that period. Interactive forums disseminated and facilitated content on behalf of Jihadi organizations but were not necessarily directly linked to the leading figures. From that phase onwards "users can play a role in posting a variety of materials, including their own views on events, and have the ability to converse with like-minded individuals across a wide geographic area." (Zelin 2013, p. 4)

In the late 2000's the control of the content shifted towards the single individual when social media platforms and user-generated content became popular and widely used. Jihadist and radical Islamic content started popping up on mainstream blogging, social-networking, video-sharing, and instant messaging platforms. Rather than being tucked away in the hidden corners of the Internet, it became possible for people to virtually stumble into extremist propaganda on sites like YouTube, Twitter, Facebook, and WordPress: "Individuals, not an organization, decide what is important and what they believe should be given the most attention." (ibid., p. 4)

Social media platforms have lower technical and financial barriers to entry, and have the added bonus of reaching much wider constituencies than is likely via a dedicated website. The arrows in the following diagram refer to information flow through the system since the establishment of electronic media.

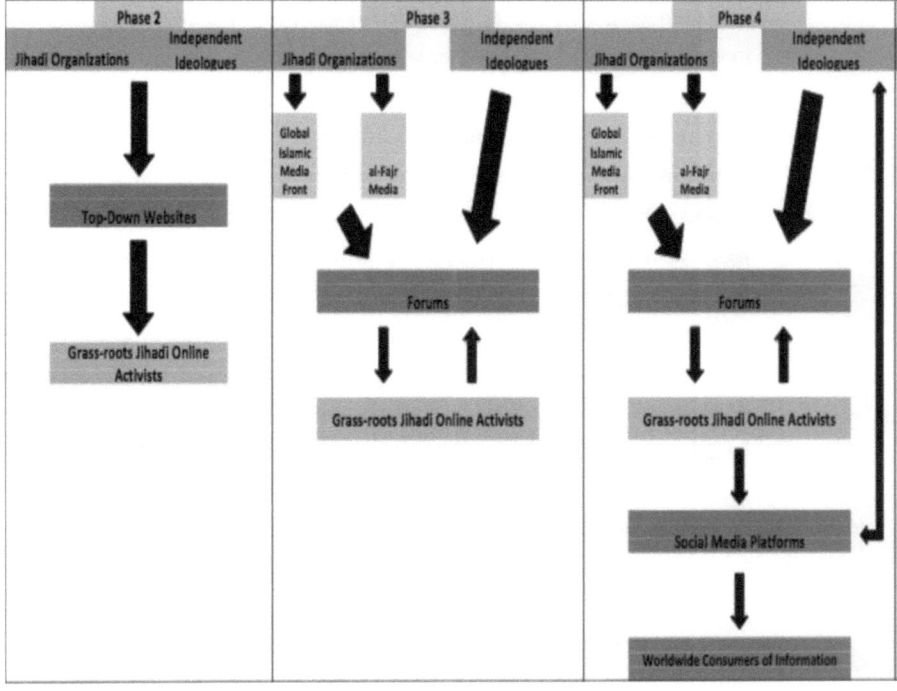

2 Zelin (2013, p. 9)

The Jihadist web presence includes interactive forums and discussion boards, venues to download and upload videos, graphic and audio files, and online question-and-answer services where members can get advice on religious or social issues. There are only a handful of virtual media organizations that create the publications or the visual propaganda material, which can then be picked up and passed on via a multitude of connected websites or social media forums. Internationally most important are "As-Sahab" which is the media production house of al-Qaeda, the "Al-Fajr" media center and the Global Islamic Media Front (Stenersen 2008, p. 222).

6.2 The transformative potential of social media

The development of Web 2.0 together with the prevalence of social media was a major change affecting the Internet, human relationships and the organization of groups. The process towards a new web era started in 1999 with the popularization of the blogging tools and the associated idea of collective publishing. The Internet of today has become a medium that is not only passively information oriented but has been used for communication and community building. Social media is a very broad term and has been defined in many different ways. The term "Web 2.0" was first coined in 2004 and primarily groups together much of the new phenomena of the Internet. One of the core elements of the definitions is that the Internet and other new technologies are moving away from a one-to-many model, for example broadcast, towards a many-to-many model, such as Twitter and Facebook. Consequently, the Salafist message that was only available to a smaller parochial audience in the past is increasingly being granted much more diffuse audience penetration. The Web 2.0 that has been used by Salafi-Jihadists in the last years includes different forms like blogging, micro-blogging, social networking, photo, video and music sharing, and even virtual worlds such as "Second Life". The "Handbook of Online and Social Media Research" specifies two elements of the Web 2.0:

> "The first is the emergence, growth, and popularity of social media; the second is a change in the paradigm of how control is shared between providers and users. The adoption of the idea of Web 2.0 reflected the evidence that users were taking more control of their interactions with media, with organizations, and with each other." (Poynter 2010, p. 161)

When Manuel Castells (2009, p. 64) says, that "[w]e do not 'watch' the Internet as we watch television", he means, that the old media-analysis of an "audience" is obsolete because today, people are not just passive recipients of news, information, norms and culture; today they have become active creators. Yochai Benkler describes the active and creative use of social production networks as a force towards an improvement of individual liberty. Each participant

> "has decided to take advantage of some combination of technical, organizational, and social conditions within which we have come to live, and to become an active creator in his or her own world, rather than merely to accept what was already there. The belief that it is possible to make something valuable happen in the world, and the practice of actually acting on that belief, represent a qualitative improvement in the condition of individual freedom. They mark the emergence of new practices of self-directed agency as a lived experience." (Benkler 2006, p. 137)

In the Foreign Affairs-article "The Political Power of Social Media", Shirky Clay (2011), an advocate for the politically transformative potential of social media, acknowledges three main effects the new Internet has on media and the public sphere. First, granting access to a tremendous amount of information; second, enabling the rise of citizen journalism and, third, enabling groups of people to synchronize their actions. When it comes to the potential of connection technologies, Clay sounds optimistic.

Contrary, there is Evgeny Morozov's book "The Net Delusion: The Dark Side of Internet Freedom" (2011). It was released right before the Tunisian revolution started and sheds a much darker light on the potential of the new Internet. He can be read as a critical corrective questioning that the Internet was inherently democratic and that social media favours the oppressed citizen. Where Shirky sees the potential in technological connectivity, Morozov (p. 260) warns that promoting Internet freedom must include measures to mitigate the negative side effects of increased interconnectedness:

> "[T]he freedom to connect, at least in its current somewhat abstract interpretation, would be a great policy priority in a democratic paradise, where citizens have long forgotten about hate, culture wars, and ethnic prejudices. But such an oasis of tolerance simply does not exist."

Along with the ability to broadcast ourselves, the Internet has allowed the user the ability to undermine the prevailing dominance of the mass media. There are more ways to spread more ideas to more people than at any moment in history. The GJM is aware of these changes. Al-Qaeda announces:

> "In this day and age, where electronic advances are quite sophisticated and the power of communication and knowledge is applied to the Internet and the Satellite television stations, both are powerful engines for communicating with the public at large (…) Let us not forget that large scale publication expenses are exorbitantly high and exceed the budgets and capabilities of most organizations, not to mention the inconceivable option of disseminating a particular jihadist ideology. The answer to overcome that difficulty lies in the Internet and the Satellite television stations that have and are visiting the critical mass of households, rich and poor." (Aaron 2008, p. 274)

A statement like this illustrates the change in the structure and make-up of the GJM organizations themselves. Gone, for the most part, are the days of clearly delineated, hierarchically-organized terrorist groups: "Today´s terrorist organization is more likely to be a network of loosely connected cells, bound by a common ideology, than a rigid military-style hierarchy with a clear-cut political goal. While the hierarchies of leadership still do exist, the modern terrorist can act with much greater autonomy than ever before." (Shahar 2005, p. 78)

6.3 The global ummah: From virtual to real-world terrorism

Social networking sites help to build a sense of community for their members, allowing them to belong to an entity greater than themselves, independent of geography or local circumstances. For Reuven Paz (2010), "the main platform for developing and pushing the culture of global jihad forward has in recent years been the Internet." (Paz 2010, p. XIVii) He lists two main reasons for this development. First, he argues, that in most Arab and Muslim countries most opposition groups are persecuted. That leaves the Internet as only vehicle for spreading their message. Second, the Internet is the best way to reach the broadest possible audience: "Every jihadi event or message is instantly exposed to the world, new agencies, and Muslim countries whose populations do not read Arabic." (Paz 2010, p. XIViii)

Brian Jenkins (2011) is one of the most renowned researchers in the field of terrorism and analyses the impact of the Internet on al-Qaeda and its important purpose for internal and external communication:

> "Terrorists use the Internet to disseminate their ideology, appeal for support spread fear and alarm among their foes, radicalize and recruit new members, provide instruction in tactics and weapons, gather intelligence about potential targets, clandestinely communicate, and support terrorist operations. The Internet enables terrorist organizations to expand their reach, create virtual communities of like-minded extremists, and capture a larger universe of more-diverse talents and skills." (B. Jenkins 2011, p. 4)

These "virtual communities of like-minded extremists" that can be described as a "global ummah" have served as an accelerator to radicalize the GJM compared to what would have been the case in the era of print media. To make this argument, Yael Shahar (2005, p. 83) quotes that this construction of the online GJM-community satisfies four criteria that are essential to the sense of community. The first criteria for Shahar is the "feeling of membership" that is a feeling of identifying with the community. Secondly, there is the "feeling of influence" in both ways: of having influence on, and being influenced by, the community. The feeling of being supported by others in the community while also supporting them is an essential point as well. Lastly, Shahar quotes a "shared emotional connection" that influences feelings of relationships, shared history, and a certain "spirit" of community. Once involved in an extremist network, powerful social psychological processes bind the individual to the group, including the emotional rewards of belonging. The British security service MI5 recognizes this role of online communities:

> "People do not generally become radicalised simply through passive browsing of extremist websites, but many such sites create opportunities for the 'virtual' social interaction that drives radicalisation in the virtual world. Books, DVDs, pamphlets and music all feature in the experiences of (…) terrorists but their emotional content – eg images of atrocities against Muslims – is often more important than their factual content.(…) Membership of a terrorist group can provide a sense of meaning and purpose. It can lead to enhanced self-esteem, and the individual can feel a sense of control and influence over their lives (…) some may find psychological security in a belief in future rewards (both in paradise and in the collective memory of the movement) following suicide operations." (Travis 2008, para. 13)

Jihadi punditry has become a critical part of the online radicalization process for both its producers and consumers. According to Brachman (2010, para. 3), the number of web Jihadists who make the transition to real-world terrorists is growing. Terrorists who have been radicalized online include Badr al-Harbi, a Kuwaiti who posted extensively on an al-Qaeda Internet forum before blowing himself up in Iraq 2008. "In doing so, [he has] taught other Web jihadists how to upgrade their keyboards into suicide vests. With his many screeds posted to forums lionizing those who carry al-Qaeda's torch, (…) [he] helped narrow the distance separating the global jihadi movement's fighters and its online sympathizers." (ibid) For Brachman, al-Harbi was an example for a jihadi pundit, leveraging his writings to achieve a prominent position within the so-called online "jihadisphere".

Social media platforms have not only enabled global jihadi entrepreneurs to share news items, original articles and nasheeds (Islamic songs) but to unite the ummah:

> "The newer technology lowered the bar for participation, making the involvement of low-level or non-Jihadis in the online conversation a new feature of the global jihad movement. Those so inclined can talk about jihad all day on the Web, even if they are geographically dispersed. This was not possible beforehand (…). The social media platforms are where the product and ideas are sold. Social media can expose the global jihadi message to anyone, whereas before, one had to knowingly want to be directly exposed to the message by going to the forums. (…) The interactive nature of social media technologies and their early adoption by online Jihadis have exposed a new generation to the global jihad." (Zelin 2013, p. 5-6)

Spreading propaganda and ideology on the Internet creates a foundation for contemporary Jihadists. However, this one-way communication is mostly accompanied by personal online contact that preserves the infrastructure of today´s loosely knit GJM (Rogan 2006, p. 25). For many of the young generation of potential radical Islamists, the establishment of virtual friendships and thereby the feeling of being a recognized part of a virtual "ummah" seems to play a significant role:

> "[The] 'Internetted' communication is of tremendous importance, in particular to supporters of jihadism, who are scattered through the world. Communication with fellow sympathizers creates a virtual community, a sense of unity and belonging to a group and a cause." (Rogan 2006, p. 25)

These virtual networks increase the speed of dissemination of radical interpretation of Quran verses, Islamist news and invocations to actions. This rapid interactive and reciprocal propaganda machinery has become an independent mechanism and is, according to Brachman, an important factor in the radicalization process. A key element of building up political and religious Islamist structures is "the creation of a unified identity on which collective action can occur." (Brachman 2009, p. 12) The single "revolutionary" deed is not directly conducted by affiliated members of a specific organization with a clear and strict hierarchy but can be accomplished by any individual from a global unity of like-minded people that are united in the feeling of affiliation, of belonging to "one ummah". In this sense, the innovative ways in which Jihadists are now using the Internet have helped open Jihadist participation to anyone.

The Jihadist websites differ in nature and are run relatively independent by different groups or individuals. Many sites however are redistributing and circulating the same material. By enforcing the pure tenets of Islam and simultaneously being very encouraged in spreading these ideas in modern and for adolescents' attractive communication channels, the Salafis pose a threat to more moderate Muslim web sites. These efforts to seek dominance over this technology and to establish or take over ideological space are an apparent motive of today's GJM:

> "Jihadist-minded individuals and organizations are increasingly looking to extend the discussion into (...) the broader Sunni community. By embedding Jihadist writings on mainstream Islamic sites, and posting Jihadist arguments on non-Jihadist web forums, proponents of this hostile ideology are providing new avenues for Muslims to engage with the ideology whereas previously they might not have had the opportunity to do so." (Brachman 2009, p. 14)

Al-Qaeda, the German Salafis and affiliated organizations consider themselves the vanguard of the struggle, "as a core group of believers that is striking a path that the rest of the Muslim ummah will follow." (Pantucci 2011, p. 11)

6.4 Forums & Facebook[15]

Forums represent a category of social media websites that are increasingly popular among Jihadists. Forums are mainly public arenas for individuals, where users make their viewpoints public and discuss almost any subject. Moreover, they reinforce the views of their members and create virtual communities that work similarly to the ones in the offline world. They are important to make connections and to share partly secret information – especially when these forums are open for members only.

As boundaries between 'consumers' and 'producers' are sometimes wide apart, forum members feel closer to social movements, especially when actively participating, contributing, and sharing content. For any organization of the GJM, web forums concomitant with anonymity in communication are providing a multifaceted platform for camouflaging clandestine activities, spreading Jihadist ideology and promoting information needed for recruiting, fundraising or instructing in military tactics.

---

[15] While Facebook is currently being used as the main platform to share ideological and operational information, it is by no means the only social networking site being employed for Jihadist use. The Islamic equivalent to Facebook is called "Milat Facebook". The Salafi Muslim Brotherhood for example has created and launched its own social networking site called Ikhwan Book (www.ikhwanweb.com).

Forums are similar to social media platforms but often provide a closed framework and are subject to internal censorship. While social media platforms operate with a certain site policy, privately installed forums with a password protection offer an open space for propaganda without denunciation of hate speech. Besides being a propaganda distribution machine, many forums are discussing electronic Jihad, where methods of hacking are discussed (Rogan 2006, p. 22).

As argued before, the very act of participating in Jihadist web forums gives individuals the experience of being part of a global brotherhood where, across national borders and continents, a real sense of community is likely to emerge. In itself, therefore, the Internet represents the sense of 'global ummah'[16], the underlying principle of much Islamist militant ideology (Sageman 2004, p. 161).

Web forums are mostly administered and populated by grassroots supporters. They are the communication centers of the Islamist militant movement, where key debates about the latest news take place and networks are formed. Often forums are password-protected and are used to exchange videos, training material, and links to other web sites and new addresses of those that already existed but were closed by authorities (Neumann & Rogers 2007, pp. 83-84).For the Jihadi Websites Monitoring Group, a group of researchers associated with the International Institute for Counter-Terrorism, the Jihadist web forums are the main platform for understanding the workings of Jihadist movements:

> "They [the forums] represent an authentic and important source of information for understanding the jihadist dialogue, jihadist propaganda efforts, religious-legal debate, dialogue about strategy, and the mood and feelings about Web surfers regarding the progress of Global Jihad." (Jihadi Websites Monitoring Group 2012, p. 2)

As Internet technology has developed, especially in the last decade, it has gained "utmost importance for al-Qaeda and other organizations of Global Jihad", especially through integrating Facebook, Twitter and other social networks as part of

---

[16] I am referring with this expression to the media theorist Marshall Mc Luhan who coined the expression of the Internet and the transition of consciousness as 'global village' (Mc Luhan 1964: *Understanding Media*. Canada: McGraw-Hill) In the same work of his from 1964 he presents the prescient maxim that "the medium is the message". His theory may help in a deeper theoretical analysis of how the promotion of a virtual Jihad within this new social media environment has recast the ideology of Jihadism.

an "electronic jihad" allowing file sharing and daily contact with their predominantly Western audiences.

> "The plethora of jihadist sites (…) bears witness to this medium's status as a modern, facile means of communication (…). Through the Internet, Al-Qaeda and its ilk transmit news, announcements, and ideology not only to the Muslim public but also, and perhaps primarily, to the Western public."
> (Jihadi Websites Monitoring Group 2012, pp. 4-5)

Social networks such as Facebook can be regarded as a form of substitution and at the same time as a supplement to the classic but not outdated form of social media: the web forum. While Jihadi forums are mostly frequented by people who have already become radicalized or support Jihad, Facebook offers a space to interact with mainstream Muslims, exchange ideas and attract new supporters

A relative disadvantage to the GJM in using forums for communication is their transparency for intelligence services. Collecting information while observing and publishing contents and shutting down these forums can make individuals more wary about their online footprint and "deter individuals from joining the movement or convince them that being involved is no longer worth the risks. " (Zelin 2013, p.2) This is likely to draw individuals into more diffuse networks

3 "No mercy with kuffar just kill them..." Facebook post by "Cholocho Weza Rohoyo" on March 3, 2013.

such as Facebook where they are not as controllable for the authorities as they were under the semi-centralized system of forums. When Jihadists leave exclusive web arenas, "they can interact with non-jihadis, they have more opportunity to recruit new individuals to the cause. This more diffuse nature, though, makes it harder for intelligence analysts to track the movement, since the activists are no longer centralized in a forum." (Zelin 2013, p.2) The mentioned American social network offers a new type of mass interpersonal persuasion and motivates individuals to contribute by uploading images, videos or by simply commenting on others.

Pursuant to Facebook Rights and Responsibilities on the website[17], "You will not post content or take any action on Facebook that infringes or violates someone else's rights or otherwise violates the law." (Paragraph 5.1) It also states that "We can remove any content or information you post on Facebook if we believe that it violates this Statement or our policies." (Paragraph 5.2)

However, information is not screened before it is posted, so posts that violate the rules remain on the site until they are detected and removed. In open Jihadist groups and on private Jihadi accounts, anti-Semitic and anti-American statements and a fundamental attitude against democracy is daily business (see chapter 3). The same counts for calls to terrorize Israel and the United States. After the bombings in Boston on April 15, 2013, Facebook pages were full of praise and sympathy with the terrorists. A person with the name "Tandhyn AlQuaedah" posted a picture[18] of both attackers commenting it with the following: "You are viewing our fellowship came to attack Obama, let's end the United States of America. so that the beginning of what we will do with America, these two brothers were not alone, then turns new attacks on Obama.. (…) so happy to know that we are meeting for the destruction of America in the name of God my brothers ALLAHUAKBAR" (original orthography) Comments followed by sympathizers praising the bravery of the two Chechen brothers. Muhammad Quassem replies in that conversation: "We have to follow these examples of courage and attack enemies".

4 Picture posted on April 19, 2013, by the Facebook group "Die Stimme der Ummah"

According to a case study by the US`s Department of Homeland Security (2010) about the terrorist use of social media, Facebook serves the following purposes:

> "As a way to share operational and tactical information, such as bomb recipes, AK-47 maintenance and use, tactical shooting, etc.; As a gateway to extremist sites and other online radical content by linking on Facebook

---

[17] Retrieved from http://www.facebook.com/note.php?note_id=10151420037600301, on April 2, 2013.
[18] Retrieved from https://www.facebook.com/photo.php?fbid=144924569021800&set=a.109776579203266.13810.100005127727059&type=1&theater on April 22, 2013.

group pages and in discussion forums; As a media outlet for terrorist propaganda and extremist ideological messaging; As a wealth of information for remote reconnaissance for targeting purposes" (para. 3)

Besides the many advantages using Facebook and Twitter for discussions and information exchange, one of the main limitations is the openness and transparency that already led to many arrests and prosecutions under charges of glorifying and abetting terrorism. Therefore it is probable that the trend for the more advanced part of the GJM is towards closed forums for communication and coordination. It is also likely that GJM members cells will adopt greater vigilance against the activities of law enforcement agencies and that they will develop more innovative ways in which to protect their communications from infiltration and monitoring.

5 Cover page of the German Salafist Facebook group "Die Stimme der Ummah" (Engl.: Voice of the ummah) with currently 4874 followers (April15, 2013)

7. Social media strategies of the German Salafi sect

Berlin, Bonn, Ulm, Neunkirchen, Essen, Langen. These German cities have among others brought up a new generation of Islamist terrorists who had not grown up abroad or were socialized within a strict Islamist community. Those radicals are German born 'homegrown' Jihadists who often radicalized within a few months (Schmidt 2012, para. 3-4).

Jihadism cannot be extricated from the religious and ideological context from which it emerged: political Islam in general and Salafism in particular. The modern Salafi movement arose in the context of gradual Muslim decadence over the past 500 years, during which Islam fell from its dominant position in the world. That decline presents a problem at various levels as it is the Islamic understanding to be the last and perfect revelation from God. Within the Muslim community, one of the explanations for the decline, from a more fundamentalist Islamic point of view, is that Muslims have strayed from the righteous path and have not practiced the faith in the right way. The revivalist version of Islam advocating a return to the authentic ancient faith is called Salafi (Sageman 2006, p.123). Considering the fact that the *global* Jihad is a distinctly modern phenomenon which has coincided with the revolution in information and communication technologies, the apparent Salafi anachronism can be regarded as a product of modernity (Sageman 2004, p. 158). No modern tool of technology is as widely associated with globalization as the Internet. The success of global Salafism does not proceed *despite* modernity, globalization and the broad use of the Internet technology, but there is a coherency. While most Muslim communities are separated by origin, Salafism is an outcome of this modernization and globalization. Salafism does not accept a nation state with its borders; it does not care about culture or language but offers a movement that can be joined easily and from everywhere disregarding social class and origin (ibid). That makes this ideology offering concrete laws and traditional role models, attractive in times of world-wide migration and identity crisis.

7.1 Salafism in Germany

The Salafis[19] are examined here as part of the GJM are a world-wide Muslim revivalist movement with the goal of establishing a great orthodox Islamic state, eliminating national boundaries and establishing 'sharia', or God´s law, on the basis of Quran and Sunna, the religious practice of Muhammed, the founder of the Islamic faith. The Islamic sect of "Salafiyyah" preaches together with the restoration of "authentic Islam", a radical anti-Western strategy of violent jihad: "The global version of this movement [the Salafis] advocates the defeat of the Western powers that prevent the establishment of a true Islamic state." (Sageman, 2004, p. 1) Violent Jihad has many faces and is regardless of its type and exact motivation no synonym for terrorism according to the definition used in this paper. It can take different forms and methods of armed struggle. A number of militant Islamist groups are foremost focused and engaged in fighting in armed regional conflicts and do not support indiscriminate attacks against civilians (Stepanova 2008, p. 86).

Whether all Salafis are immediate sympathizers of terror or not, they are acting ideologically and practically in a sphere, in which using terrorism – in its modern and new form – is seen as an option or opportunity to achieve their purposes. According to the German domestic security agency, the "Verfassungsschutz" (office for the protection of the constitution), there are two different streams in the Salafi movement, the "political wing" and the "Jihadist wing". The political Salafism tries to gain attention and influence through intense propaganda, the so-called "Da`wa" (Arabic: making an invitation). Adherents of the Jihadi Salafism are directly propagating and using violence to achieve their goals. Transitions between the two streams which are using the same religious authorities and masterminds are fluent as analyses of radicalization processes show. They solely differ in the choice of their actions to achieve their common goal. Almost all identified terrorist structures and persons developed from the Salafi milieu[20].

---

[19] Not all Salafis are actively militant. For more detailed distinctions amongst followers of the Salafi movement, see Quintan Wiktorowicz (2006), *Anatomy of the Salafi Movement*, Studies in Conflict and Terrorism, 29(3), pp. 207-39.
[20] See: Bundesamt für Verfassungsschutz (2013): *Islamismus und islamistischer Terrorismus*. Retrieved from: http://www.verfassungsschutz.de/de/arbeitsfelder/af_islamismus/salafistische_bestrebungen/ on January 28, 2013.

The German Salafis are most notably represented by single spiritual ideologues and the groups "Die wahre Religion" (Engl.: The true religion) and "Einladung zum Paradies" (Engl.: Invitation to paradise) which are two of the Salafi groups under surveillance by German security authorities. According to F. W. Horst (2012, para. 1), the Salafi movement has become not only a fundamentalist way of interpreting Islam but an unprecedented "counter-culture" of primarily young adults missionizing for the Salafi-Wahabi faith and rejecting enlightenment and Western civilization. For Salafis, the Islamic rules are an entire guideline for all aspects in life. From picking eye brows that is haram (forbidden) according to Salafi rule[21], to family life, the right cloth, to eating habits and subsequent dental care, the everyday life voluntarily subjected to the "law of Allah". There are ideological and personal ramifications (General Anzeiger Bonn 2013, January 26) to the 2012 banned association of "Millatu Ibrahim" (Faith of Ibrahim). According to Burkhard Freier, head of the German domestic secret service, the "Verfassungsschutz" of the state of North Rhine-Westphalia, the number of "fanatic Islamist" in the state, most of them Salafis, have doubled, now there are around 1000 of them, country-wide there are an estimated 5000: "German establishments are still in the firing line of Islamist terrorists." (Rp-online, 2013 January 10) According to the security service, 20 members of the German Salafi movement joined al-Qaida in Pakistani training camps in 2012.

7.2 The Salafi use of social media

Social networks as Facebook and video platforms as YouTube are being used by the Salafis to spread a segregating and violence-glorifying ideology. "Google is full of Salafism" states Florian Flade (2012, para. 7): "Young Muslims that are searching for Islamic topics are likely to hit Salafi webpages that do not leave any space for interpretation."

German Jihadists focus primarily on offering and distributing Jihadist information and material, often via free websites, such as WordPress-domains. This information concerns, among other things, literature translated into German language about waging Jihad against non-believers, statements by radical Islamic groups, or adding

---

[21] See: Abu Dujana (2010, July 10): *Ist Augenbrauen zupfen Haram*. Retrieved from: http://www.youtube.com/watch?v=qZn7vKeYtDE on February 4th, 2013.

subtitles for example to al-Qaeda video productions. The use of free web spaces appeared to be attractive because it scarcely required any registration, and offered anonymity. Since June 2012, however, there are more restrictions by German authorities against Salafi groups and their websites. In March 2013, German authorities put a ban on "Dawa Ffm", one of the leading propaganda portals of the scene. They are accused of turning against the value order, to reject the rule of law and to seek an order under the laws of the Islamic sharia. They are also calling for violence against dissenters (Tretbar 2013, para. 2).

There are a handful of virtual media organizations that play an important role in creating Jihadist audience. The organizations are more important than the actual web sites or hosts as these are under permanent surveillance for infringements. Many of the sites have been blocked perpetually and appeared under a new alias with a new host and address.

7.2.1. Global Islamic Media Front

The popularization of the online Jihadist movement empowered organizations dedicated to translating materials, in most cases from Arabic to English or German. The Global Islamic Media Front (GIMF) as a prominent media organ of al-Qaida was a key innovator in this regard (Zelin 2013, p. 5). How the international GIMF distributes its videos and manifests shows a figure from the FBI (Reid 2009, para. 14):

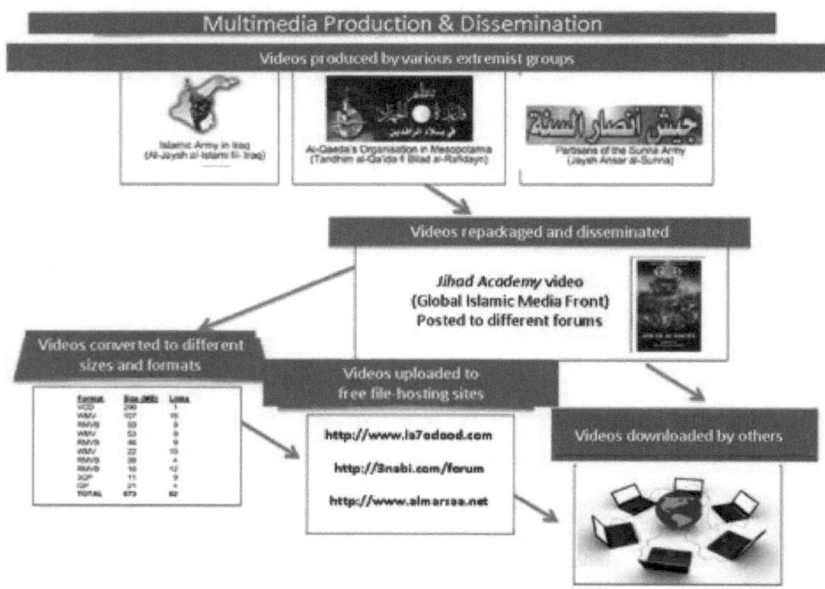

The "Global Islamic Media Front – Abteilung für Fremdsprachen und Übersetzung" (section of foreign languages and translation) appears in the German speaking Internet as a platform translating Arabic al-Qaida linked material into German language. Head of the German speaking branch of the GIMF is Mohamed Mahmoud[22], a central ideological leader of the militant Jihadist struggle for the German audience and head of the in 2012 prohibited German group "Millatu-Ibrahim". The directly and offensive militant Salafi group "Millatu Ibrahim" appeared with a direct militant approach. Their speeches were characterized by a clear and unambiguous language aiming to motivate young Muslims to join the Jihadist struggle. The German Penal Code prohibits hate speech and utterances capable instigating violence, hatred or discrimination. Many Jihadist sites therefore shift to American host servers

Mahmoud with his Islamic alias Abu Usama al-Gharib, was born in 1985 and is son of Egyptian parents. He grew up in Austria where he was jailed for four years for

---

[22] For data security reasons I will anonymize the real names but apply the clear name when it comes to people who are either in the public eye or when self-chosen Islamic names (Arabic: kunya) that are pseudonyms are used.

supporting al-Qaida. After his release, he moved to Egypt where he teamed up with other German Salafis that had left Germany into Islamic countries. From Egypt they are distributing through these channels: inflammatory pamphlets, hate sermons, written and spoken material. A threatening video was released in February 2013 in which the German chancellor Angela Merkel received death threats by the German with the Islamic name "Abu Azzam the German", a fellow of the Mahmoud-group. In this "nasheed", Abu Azzam calls for the death of Barak Obama and Angela Merkel: "Osama [bin Laden; the author] wait for us because we have tasted blood. We want to see Obama and Merkel dead." (Flade 2013, Feb. 2)

6 "Märtyrer Operationen" Propaganda material by GIMF distributed via social media platforms

The Jihadist songs on YouTube primarily try to stir up a feeling of anger against the West among Muslims, and to incite them to take action. These so-called "nasheeds" are an important propaganda instrument that could be described as an Islamic rap song. They project a romantic image of the violent Jihad.

On March 15, Mohammed released a YouTube video[23] published by his organization GIMF under the title "Die Staatsbürgerschaft der Kreuzzügler ist unter meinen Füßen" (Engl.: The citizenship of the crusaders is under my feet). In that 11 minutes video, Mahmoud appears with his Islamic name Abu Usama Al-Gharib and proclaims that he is not a citizen of Austria anymore. To confirm his words, he tears his passport in pieces and burns it. Mahmoud says:

> "I´m not an Austrian, I´m a Muslim and only part of the ummah. That´s why I declare today the renunciation of the Austrian citizenship. (…) I´m not part of this Aids-contaminated society. I´m a Mujahed [Arabic: struggler /mean.: soldier for Allah] that aims to slaughter this laicism and these dogs (…). With the help of Allah, I will prevail over them and chip off their heads."
> (Min. 04:28 - 6:08)

---

[23] http://www.youtube.com/watch?v=NYlswpvvvGU on March 16, 2013.

With his open calls in German language for violent action, Mahmoud is a role model for German Jihadi Salafists. In an interview with him that was published by the GIMF with the title "Abrechnung mit Deutschland" (transl.: Judging Germany), Mahmoud calls for the killing of members of the German right-wing party "Pro-NRW". On March 12, authorities arrested a conspirative cell of Jihadists with strong Salafi ties for planning the murder of the head of the "Pro NRW"-party (Flade, March 16).

7 "Abrechnung mit Deutschland" Magazine of the GIMF in German language to download via Jihadi web-forums

Another nasheed-video, produced by the former German rap-artist "Deso Dogg", who emigrated to Egypt as part of Mahmoud's GIMF, declares holy war on Germany after Salafi clashes with police in the German city of Solingen because of displayed "Mohammed caricatures" by Pro NRW members:

> "No doubt about it. Islam will prevail and the victory is already very close (…) We warn you Pro NRW. Take heed, when you go to sleep at night! (…) Stay fit, do a lot of sports, prepare your body (…) In Germany, we will make the ground shake and only for Allah (…) Hail stones will rain on the kuffar [unbelievers] because they do not fear Allah (…) War and death will come to Germany, car bombs will explode! You have been warned, but you have ignored. They will come from all over the world to die, they are the chosen (…) We are fighting democracy, the biggest lie of the kuffar. The noble sword of Sharia has come to win here. No end in sight, we bring war and death to your front door." (Kern 2013, para. 30)

7.2.2 Die Wahre Religion – The true religion

Videos published on YouTube are a modern pillar of indoctrination and call for example for separation from the kufar (the non-believers). In a video[24] entitled "Abu Ibrahim und Abu Dujana (Sylvester Haram - Iserlohn)" uploaded on January 22, 2013, by the German Salafi channel "Indyjournalists", the protagonist with the Islamic name Abu Ibrahim, agitates against democracy and secularists in a simplistic manner: "How many of our sisters are out there today? How many sisters will walk

---

[24] www.youtube.com/watch?v=AGrg7fezRAk, accessed on March 2, 2013.

out half-naked? How many brothers are out there to hold the hand of an alien woman? How many sisters of ours are selling themselves in a cheap manner?" (min. 03:55-04:14)

Abu Ibahim is part of the group "Die wahre Religion". His speech is exemplary as he presents a dichotomic weltanschauung and sets own respectively Islamic moral standards that seem superior to the non-believers whose destiny it is to literally go to hell. This is the ideology of Jihadist militants wrapped in legitimizing words of an ostensible Islamic pundit. For Claudia Dantschke, a German expert on Islamism, the dangerous potential of such groups as "Die wahre Religion" which she claims are legitimizing militant action, lies in their influence on non-radical Muslims. They would be the main target for their propaganda (Kuhlmann 2013, para. 9).

8. Modern Jihadist characters and the influence of the Internet on the Salafist scene

"We strongly urge Muslim Internet professionals to spread and disseminate news and information about the jihad through e-mail lists, discussion groups and their own Web sites (...). The more Web sites, the better it is for us. We must make the Internet our tool." (al-Qaeda, in Aaron 2008, p. 274)

This quote of one of the leading al-Qaeda members calls for the organized, strategic exploitation of the Internet, recognizing its value as a platform for reaching a wider, younger audience. Together with the cases explained further above it demonstrates how Islamist content catering for Western audiences through Web 2.0 has been made increasingly accessible and finds a crowd of recipients; people who stumble across extremist content by accident or people who are looking for those contents and build up links to either radical, open or clandestine organizations. Despite the common consensus that real-world social relationships continue to be decisive and personal bonds as group-dynamics are an important part in the process of radicalization (Neumann & Rogers 2007 , pp. 66-81 and Lützinger 2012, pp. 20-37), there are cases in which individuals have become indoctrinated in relative isolation. The Internet-mediated forms of interaction can constitute a genuine form of social interaction and can act as an acceptable substitute for interpersonal socialization.

The easy availability of extremist material due to the increasing prevalence of the Internet has fostered the growth of the autodidactic extremist. It is therefore likely that the Internet has not only changed the process of radicalization but also exercised a certain influence on the nature of terrorism and will continue to do so in the future.

8.1 Loners, Lone Wolves, Lone Wolf Pack and Lone Attackers

The network of individuals connected through the Internet allows determined individuals to "self-radicalize". Marc Sageman (2008) calls these new instances of a so-called "lone wolf terrorism" a phenomenon of "leaderless jihad". A German case from March 2011 can serve as an elucidative example: Arid Uka fatally shot two US soldiers who were boarding a bus at the Frankfurt airport and severely wounded others. According to the prosecutors, Uka had seen a video on YouTube purporting to show Muslim women being raped by US soldiers. The then 21-years old man studied videos of radical preachers, frequented Islamist discussion forums online and had a Facebook account with several friends from the German Salafi scene. However, he never had direct personal contact with them and was never involved in a physical network. According to Guido Steinberg, a German researcher on Salafism and Islamist terrorism, the language barrier to propaganda written in Arabic was very high in Germany till the Internet offered a wide array of translations. Uka used very sophisticated German-language propaganda online and especially Islamist videos as those by the GIMF described further above have shown their effectiveness, argues Steinberg and sees in the radicalization process of the young Jihadist a reminder that terrorist groups are able to persuade their followers remotely, with no physical contact (Jansen 2011, para. 3-5).

Raffaello Pantucci (2011) differentiates between four different typologies of lone terrorists: the Loner, the Lone Wolf, the Lone Wolf Pack, and the Lone Attacker. These types are in contrast to terrorism organized by a network of active extremists, either connected to Al Qaeda or one of its regional synonyms. This autodidactic element within the research of Islamist terrorism complicates matters from an analytical perspective.

> "The autodidactic element adds a complicating factor (…) [T]he loner who seeks attention through an act of terrorism (…) can quite quickly claim to be an Islamist warrior by quoting Osama bin Laden or using the widely available terminology associated with jihad (…) This is something that has been increasingly facilitated by the growth of the Internet and the availability of Al Qaeda ideology online (…)" (Pantucci 2011, p. 12)

The individuals within the group of the "Loner" attempt to carry out or prepare for a terrorist incident and deploy an Islamist justification for their action. "[W]hile he (or she) may utilize the ideological cover of an Islamist ideology to provide an explanation for their action, they do not appear to have any actual connection or contact with extremists beyond what they are able to access through passive consumption on the Internet or from society at large." (Pantucci 2011, p. 14) They carry out their actions without external command or control.

The term "Lone Wolf" terrorist is used to refer to individuals pursuing Islamist terrorist goals alone, either driven by personal reasons or their belief that they are part of an ideological group. In contrast to the Loner, the Lone Wolf has some level of contact with members of a terrorist organization and is

> "possibly even in contact with such individuals through the Internet in what can appear to be some sort of command and control structure. (…) While appearing to carry out their actions alone and without any physical outside instigation, [Lone Wolves] demonstrate some level of contact with operational extremists." (Pantucci 2011, pp. 19-20)

The term Lone Wolf is expanded out to "Lone Wolf Pack" when referring to small isolated groups pursuing the goal of Islamist terrorism together under the same ideology, but without the sort of external direction from an organized group or militant network (Pantucci 2011, p. 24 ff.).

The last type Pantucci (2011, p. 29 ff) mentions is a more traditional one: the "Lone Attacker". Lone Attackers are individuals who operate alone, but demonstrate clear command and links with Jihadist groups. Unlike the types introduced before, this kind of extremist has direct contact with active extremists, rather than loose online connections.

8.2 Al-Qaeda´s magazine and the recruitment of "self-made" Jihadists

From breaking news of the recent hot-spots of Islamist struggle, links to attack videos or statements of international militants to motivational imagery of martyr operatives and any kind of justifications for waging violent Jihad against the West, the German and English speaking Internet is full of any kind of propaganda. It is certain that the Internet plays an important role in recruiting new Jihadists.

There is evidence that Jihadist networks are eager to focus on Lone Wolves as a tactical tool to attack the West. Al Qaida`s "Inspire" magazine is a quarterly publication that is produced in English and Arabic and is aimed at Muslims living in the West. Shiraz Maher (2011, para. 4) summarizes the new approach with "Inspire": "First, it primes sympathetic Muslims with anti-Western anger; then it provides theological arguments which legitimize terrorism – before it finally offers detailed technical instructions on how to commit acts of terrorism."

Until his death in 2011, Anwar al-Awlaki, a radical cleric with American background was the founder and one of the editors of "Inspire". He called the strategy of his magazine an "open source jihad":

> "A resource manual for those who loath the tyrants; includes bomb making techniques, security measures, guerrilla tactics, weapons training and all other jihad related activities (…) the open source jihad is America's worst nightmare. It allows Muslims to train at home instead of risking a dangerous travel abroad." (Maher 2011, para. 5)

In actively recruiting new members for the militant struggle, "Inspire" uses most modern techniques. According to the Wire magazine, recruiting Lone Wolf terrorists is a main feature of the GJM to conduct attacks:

> "The new issue of the group's English-language online magazine, Inspire, launches a feature called the 'Convoy of Martyrs'. Complete with e-mail addresses and public encryption keys, al-Qaida in the Arabian Peninsula seeks to recruit 'lone wolf' terrorists to pull off attacks against – in order of priority – 'American targets; Israeli targets; French targets; British targets; [and] apostate regimes targets in the Muslim lands [sic]'. (…) To qualify, you must be a Muslim; must possess 'maturity'; and be skilled in 'listening and obeying'. The terrorist group provides a public encryption key and a handful of Gmail, Yahoo and Hotmail accounts where you can send your idea about who or what you'd like shoot, stab or detonate. If you're approved, off you go to kill infidels, unencumbered by any traditional terrorist cell." (Ackermann 2012, para. 3-5)

For Jenkins (2011), the Internet can actually lower the threshold of joining the Jihadi community on the one hand but on the other hand it can also serve as a distraction and prevent the cyber supporter from actually carrying out a militant operation:

> "It appears that while Internet strategies aimed at creating at least weak ties among a large number of online participants (…) to terrorist enterprises like al Qaeda, such strategies also appear to have inherent weaknesses. They may create virtual armies, but these armies remain virtual. They rely on individual initiative to carry out terrorist actions, but they offer online participants the means to vicariously participate in the campaign and please God without incurring any personal risk. Online jihadist forums may be providing an outlet that distracts jihadists from involvement in real world operations (…).For the virtual warrior, the opportunity to display one's

convictions, demonstrate one's intentions and prowess through boasts, threats, and fantasy attacks on the Internet counts as achievement (…)." (B. Jenkins 2011, p. 7)

All this focuses attention on the role played by the Internet in radicalizing individuals. Through sophisticated and password-protected web forums, al-Qaeda is now able to prime sympathizers with everything they need to become active terrorists (Maher 2011, para. 12). The aforementioned study of the New York Police Department (2007) categorizes four main categories in which the Internet can be seen as a driver and enabler for the process of radicalization:

"• In the Self-Identification phase, the Internet provides the wandering mind (…) with direct access to unfiltered radical and extremist ideology.
• It also serves as an anonymous virtual meeting place – a place where virtual groups of like-minded and conflicted individuals can meet, form virtual relationships and discuss (…) the jihadi-Salafi message they have encountered.
• During the Indoctrination phase, when individuals adopt this virulent ideology, they begin interpreting the world from this newly-formed context (…)[T]he Internet allows the aspiring jihadist to view the world and global conflicts through this extremist lens, further reinforcing the objectives and political arguments of the jihadi-Salafi agenda.
• In the Jihadization phase, when an individual commits to jihad, the Internet serves as an enabler – providing broad access to an array of information on targets, their vulnerabilities and the design of weapons." (p. 8-9)

Most of the important real-world participants in the Jihadist movement, the leadership of the various groups, the radical imams etc., are represented on the Internet; not just on static websites but on interactive web forums and so-called distributor sites where they can up- and download videos and exchange links to the current main sites that were taken down or changed its location (Neumann 2009, p. 53). Peter Neumann (54 f.) distinguishes two principal ways in which the Internet has come to be used in the process of joining the Islamist militant movement: "Internet-supported recruitment" and "self-recruitment". Talking about Internet-supported recruitment, Neumann states, that "[m]ost experts reject the notion of Internet-lead recruitment" when it comes to a recruitment for militancy because concrete social networks are required when engaging in violence or crime. He argues, that for an involvement in militant action, a certain process of socialization is necessary, in which perceptions of self-interest diminish and the value of group loyalties and personal ties increases. This corresponds with the argument of the former advisor to the US-government, Marc Sageman (2004, p. 163) that, "for the type of allegiance that the jihad demands, there is no evidence that the Internet is persuasive enough by itself."

Jarret Brachmam (2009) terms such extremists 'jihobbyists', as they are not direct members of terrorist organizations, yet actively seek to propel an radical Islamist agenda forward. Jihobbyists are both consumers and producers of Jihadist content, and they think of themselves as active and valued members of their movements who make important contributions to the struggle without being an active combatant or terrorist: "For many young men who grew up with the Internet, there is no sharp line dividing the real world from the virtual world – the virtual world *is* the real world. Online jihadism, then, may be a distraction from the real thing – not a call to arms, but a psychologically rewarding videogame." (B. Jenkins 2011, p.7)

Also Horst (2012, para. 86) acknowledges the great importance of the Internet for Islamization, radicalization and promotion of Jihad but states that the Salafist network in Germany still relies on real meeting points and the promotion of its agenda to a wider public, with public lectures, the free distribution of the Quran or demonstrations.

9. Conclusion

Over the last ten years the Internet has become increasingly important to the global Salafist movement and has been actively used for various terrorist activities. Although the use of the Internet is contested among some spiritual leaders within the Islamist community, the advantages for the loose and de-centralized transnational network of the GJM are obvious. The Internet has offered new ways in which to promote terrorism or Jihad, and thus facilitated its intensification. This work illustrates that Jihadism online has had tremendous significance in the last ten years within the GJM and its importance will most likely rise in the future, as improved bandwidth, increased functionality, and the fast growing number of users will make the Internet a far more vital nerve in modern society than it is today. The Internet and social media – as analysed in chapters 7 and 8 – are part of today's new battlefield. It can facilitate terrorist recruitment with propaganda materials, social influences, instructions in tactics and weapons and other factors. It appears difficult to state how much direct recruitment takes place on the web but it is likely that direct invitations to take part in a terrorist organization are usually delivered face-to-face. As shown through the analysis of the Salafi social media groups there is no doubt that the web is playing an important role in indoctrinating recruits before they are drawn in. It has been shown that security agencies and national authorities monitoring the cyber space are becoming more and more sensible to direct calls for Jihadist action. For that reason, Salafi-Jihadist websites and social media spaces do not attempt to recruit overtly for violent action, but instead legitimate the actions of terrorists and encourage readers to support the Jihad wherever they can.

After the elimination of Osama bin Laden and other meaningful Islamist leaders, al- Qaida and the GJM seemed weakened – with the rise of the ISIS, the "Islamic State of Iraq and the Levant" global jihadism seems more powerful and organized than ever before. The ideology is wide-spread, but the militant appearance in the West is still based on individual action rather than on a collective approach. The attempt to give responsibility to individual self-made Jihadists, so-called Lone-Wolves, is based on the organizational capabilities of the GJM in the West. Jihadism has become cloudier in the last decade: Today everyone can be a part of the movement, anywhere. As pointed out in chapter 6, the act of participating in the online "Jihadisphere" gives individuals the experience of being involved in a global brotherhood where, across national borders and continents, a real sense of community is likely to emerge. In itself, therefore, the Internet represents the sense of 'global ummah', the underlying principle of much Islamist militant ideology. The spirit of being part of this clandestine revolutionary collective, the absolute – because God-given – moral legitimacy for actions and brotherhood in the virtual and physical 'ummah' have an essential power in creating further characteristics and affiliated groups in one united Jihadist struggle. The Internet-mediated forms of communication can constitute a genuine form of social interaction and can act as an acceptable substitute for interpersonal socialization. Furthermore, the easy availability of extremist material due to the increasing prevalence of the Internet has fostered the growth of the autodidactic extremist. It is therefore likely that the Internet has not only changed the process of radicalization but also exercised influence on the nature of new terrorism.

As examined in this paper, the Internet is a decisive factor when it comes to the dissemination of ideology and radicalization but yet, its impact is quantitative rather than qualitative; the Internet has made communication safer, easier and more seamless; it has increased reaction time, provided greater scale and interactivity. In social media forums however, the vast size, the linguistically and culturally diverse user base, and lack of verification of user supplied biographical information make monitoring and evaluation of potential threats extremely difficult. Online activities need to be understood in conjunction with offline events – they remain a real-world phenomenon and cannot be dealt with simply by observing and restricting that sphere. Countering Salafist ideology comprehensively as a breeding ground for terrorism will necessarily employ a mixture of military, intelligence, financial and political instruments. The most fundamental level however is the battle of values and ideas. That means a clear condemnation of Islamist activities of any kind, the strengthening of liberal Muslim communities and isolation respectively prosecution of "spiritual leaders" preaching a violent Islam. An important accomplishment would be to spread awareness about online radicalization among parents, teachers, and Muslim community leaders, so they are able to detect, report, and – if necessary – intervene in processes of online radicalization. This work has illuminated some basic developments, different dimensions and inspirations of the global ideology of the Jihadist movement that are related to new media innovations and modifications of the communicational structure, but it is adequate in neither breadth nor depth. It would be worthwhile to intensify this study as well as to relate it to different other social media platforms and those of other language. Not only countering Salafism, Jihadism and Islamism that are dominating the contemporary coverage of Islam through their calls for radical social change and violence but the thorough study of political Islam in general as a major feature of the 21st century´s world, will be a matter of the utmost importance for many years to come.

10. References

Aaron, David (2008): *In Their Own Words. Voices of Jihad.* Sanata Monica: Rand Corporation

Adorno, Theodor W.; Horkheimer, Max (2002): *Dialectic of Enlightenment. Philosophical Fragments.* [1947] Stanford: University Press

Ackermann, Spencer (2012): *E-Mail Now and You Could Be Al-Qaida's Next Terrorist.* In: Wired Magazine. Retrieved from www.wired.com/dangerroom/ 2012/05/qaida-crowdsourcing/?utm_source=feedburner& utm_medium=feed&utm_campaign=Feed%3A+wired%2Findex+%28Wired%3A+I ndex+3+%28Top+Stories+2%29%29 on March 12, 2013.

Benkler, Yochai (2006): *The Wealth of Networks. How Social Production Transforms Markets and Freedom.* New Haven and London: Yale University Press

Beyer, Peter (1994): *Religion and Globalization.* London: SAGE Publications

Brachman, Jerret (2009): *Global Jihadism. Theory and Practice.* New York: Routledge

Brachman, Jerret (2010, January 22): *Al Qaeda`s Armies of One. Meet the next generation of Islamic pundits.* Retrieved from: www.foreignpolicy.com/articles/2010/01/22/al_qaedas_armies_of_one, on February 2, 2013.

Chomsky, Noam (2002): *Who are the Global Terrorists?* In: Booth, Ken & Tim Dunne (Eds.): *Worlds in Collision: Terror and the Future Global Order.* Basingstoke: Palgrave Macmillan

Croitoru, Joseph (2007): *Hamas. Der Islamische Kampf um Palästina.* München: C.H. Beck

Curran, James (2002): *Media and Power.* London: Routledge

Flade, Florian (2012, November 9): *Die Salafistische Verführung in Deutschland.* In: Die Welt, p. 7

Flade, Florian (2013, Feb. 2): *Islamisten drohen "Wir wollen Merkel tot sehen"* In: Die Welt. Retrieved from: www.welt.de/politik/deutschland/article113328134/Islamisten-drohen-Wir-wollen-Merkel-tot-sehen.html on February 10, 2013.

Friedman, Thomas L. (2005): *The World Is Flat. A Brief History of the Twenty-First Century.* New York: Picador

Gabler, Neal (2001, October 7): *An Eternal War of Mind-Sets.* In: Los Angeles Times. Retrieved from: http://articles.latimes.com/2001/oct/07/opinion/op-54386/3 on January 28th, 2013.

Ganor, Boaz (2005): *The Counter-Terrorism Puzzle: A Guide for Decision-Makers.* New Brunswick: Transaction Publishers

Giddens, Anthony (2009): *Sociology.* Cambridge: Polity Press

Hoffman, Bruce (1997): *Terrorism and WMD. Some Preliminary Hypotheses.* In: The Non-Proliferation Review, Spring-Summer 1997.

Horkheimer, Max (1947): *Eclipse of Reason.* New York: Oxford University Press

Huntington, Samuel P. (1993): *The Clash of Civilizations?* In: Foreign Affairs, Vol.72, No.3

Jansen, Klaus (2011, November 5): *Jihadist Internet Propaganda on the Rise.* Retrieved from: http://www.dw.de/jihadist-Internet-propaganda-on-the-rise/a-16355218 on February 2, 2013.

Jenkins, Brian Michael (2011): *Is Al Qaida's Internet Strategy Working?* Testimony presented before the Committee on Homeland Security Subcommittee on Counterterrorism and Intelligence at the United States House of Representatives on December 6, 2011. Retrieved from: www.rand.org/content/dam/rand/pubs/testimonies/2011/RAND_CT371.pdf on January 23, 2013.

Jenkins, Philip (2003): *Images of Terror. What We Can and Can't Know About Terrorism.* Berlin: De Gruyter

Kelly, Kevin (2009): *The New Socialism*. Wired magazine, June 2009

Kern, Soeren (2013, March 15): *Germany vs. Radical Islamists*. New York: Gatestone Institute

Krueger, Alan B.; Maleckova, Jitka (2003): *Education, Poverty and Terrorism: Is There a Causal Connection?* In: Journal of Economic Perspectives – Volume 17, Number 4 – Fall 2003

Kuhlmann, Jan (2013, February 1): *Salafismus als Jugendphänomen*. Retrieved from: www.dradio.de/dlf/sendungen/tagfuertag/1996413/ on March 3, 2013.

Laqueur, Walter (2000): *The New Terrorism: Fanaticism and the Arms of Mass Destruction*. Oxford: University Press

Lützinger, Saskia (2012): *The Other Side of the Story. A qualitative study of the biographies of extremists and terrorists*. Wiesbaden: Polizei und Forschung, vol. 40

Maher, Shiraz (2011, Nov 25): *„Inspire" Magazine: Open Source Jihad*. New York: Gatestone Institute

Markovits, Andrei S. (2004): *Amerika, dich haßt sich`s besser. Antiamerikanismus und Antisemitismus in Europa*. Hamburg: Konkret-Verlag

Martin, Gus (2011): *Essentials of Terrorism. Concepts and Controversies*.California: Sage Publications

Marx, Karl (2008): The 18th Brumaire of Louis Bonaparte [1852]. Maryland: Wildslide Press

Moghaddam, F.M. (2005): *The Staircase to Terrorism: A Psychological Exploration*. In: American Psychologist, 60, p. 161-169

Morozov, Evgeny (2011): *The Net Delusion. How not to liberate the world*. London: Penguin Group

Murden, Simon (2011): *Culture in World Affairs*. In: Baylis, John; Smith, Steve & Patricia Owens: *The Globalization of World Politics – An Introduction to International Relations*. Oxford: University Press

Munson, Henry Jr. (1988): *Islam and Revolution in the Middle East.* New Haven/London: Yale University Press

Najjar, Fauzzi (2005): *The Arabs, Islam and Globalization.* In: Middle East Policy, Vol. XII, No.3.

National Coordinator for Counterterrorism (2010): Jihadis and the Internet. Amsterdam: Ministry of Justice

Neumann, Peter R. (2009): *Joining Al Qaeda – Jihadist Recruitment in Europe.* New York: Routledge

Neumann, Peter R. & Brooke Rogers (2007): *Recruitment and Mobilization for the Islamist Militant Movement in Europe.* A study carried out by King's College London for the European Commission. London: King's College ICSR

Nemo, Philippe (2005): *Was ist der Westen?* Tübingen: Mohr Siebeck

Paz, Reuven (2010): *Global Jihad.* In: Rubin, Barry. Guide to Islamist Movements. New York/London: M.E. Shape

Pantucci, Raffaello (2011): *A Typology of Lone Wolve: Preliminary Analysis of Lone Islamist Terrorists.* London: ICSR

Poynter, Ray (2010): *The Handbook of Online and Social Media Research. Tools and Techniques for Market Researchers.* West Sussex: Wiley

Rabasa, Angel et al. (2006): *Beyond al-Qaeda. Part 1. The Global Jihadist Movement.* In: Rand Corporation - Project Air Force

Reid, Edna (2009): *Analysis of Jihadi Extremist Group Videos.* Forensic Sciences Communications. July 2009, Volume 11, Number 3. Retrieved from: www.fbi.gov/about-us/lab/forensic-science-communications/fsc/july2009/index.htm/
research_tech/2009_07_research01.htm on March 2, 2013.

Rubin, Barry (2010): *An Introduction to Assessing Contemporary Islamism.* In: Guide to Islamist Movements. Edited by: Barry Rubin, 2010. New York: M.E. Sharpe

Rogan, Hanna (2006): *Jihadism Online. A study of how al-Qaida and radical Islamist groups use the Internet for terrorist purposes.* Retrieved from: www.cleanitproject.eu/wp-content/uploads/2012/07/2007-jihadism-online.pdf on February 8th, 2013.

Roger, Philip (2006): *The American Enemy: The History of French Anti-Americanism.* Chicago: University Press

Sageman, Marc (2004): *Understanding Terror Networks.* Pennsylvania: University Press

Sageman, Marc (2006): *Islam and al-Qaeda.* In: Pedahzur, Ami (Ed.) : *Root Causes of Suicide Terrorism. The Globalization of Martyrdom.* London and New York: Routledge.

Sageman, Marc (2008): *Leaderless Jihad. Terror Networks in the Twenty-First Century*, Philadelphia: University Press.

Schmidt, Wolf (2012, March 23): *Die Dschihad-Jugend.* In: Die Tageszeitung (TAZ). Retrieved from: http://www.taz.de/Islamismus-in-Deutschland/!90234/ on January 28, 2013.

Shahar, Yael (2005): *The Global Jihad as Cult. Implications for Threat Assessment.* In: Ganor, Boaz & Eitan Azani (Ed.): *Trends in International Terrorism and Counter-Terrorism.* Herzliya: International Institute for Counter-Terrorism

Shirky, Clay (2011*): The Political Power of Social Media. Technology, the Public Sphere, and Political Change.* Foreign Affairs, Article from January/February 2011

Stenersen, Anne (2008): *The Internet. A Virtual Training Camp?* In: *Terrorism and Political Violence.* London and New York: Routledge

Stepanova, Ekaterina (2008): *Terrorism in Asymmetric Conflict: Ideological and Structural Aspects.* Oxford: University Press

Tapscott, Don; Williams, Anthony D. (2006): *Wikinomics. How Mass Collaboration Changes Everything.* New York: Penguin Group

Tibi, Bassam (2002): *Die fundamentalistische Herausforderung – Der Islam und die Weltpolitik*. München: C.H. Beck

Travis, Alan (2008, August 20): *The Making Of An Extremist*. In: The Guardian. Retrieved from: http://www.guardian.co.uk/uk/2008/aug/20/uksecurity.terrorism, on April 27, 2013.

Tretbar, Christian (2013, March 13): *Innenminister Friedrich geht gegen Salafisten vor*. In: Tagesspiegel. Retrieved from: http://www.tagesspiegel.de/politik/salafisten-polizei-verhindert-mordanschlag-auf-pro-nrw-chef/7919646.html on March 13, 2013.

Weimann, Gabriel (2004): *How Modern Terrorism Uses The Internet*. In: United States Institute for Peace, Washington, Special Report 116, March 2004.

Zehnpfennig, Dr. Barbara (2013, January 21): *Strukturlose Öffentlichkeit. Warum mehr Transparenz per Internet zu weniger Demokratie führen kann*. In: Frankfurter Allgemeine Zeitung, p. 7.

Zelin, Aaron Y. (2013, January): *The State of Global Jihad Online. A Qualitative, Quantitative, and Cross-Lingual Analysis*. New America Foundation at the Washington Institute. Retrieved from: www.washingtoninstitute.org/uploads/Documents/opeds/Zelin20130201-NewAmericaFoundation.pdf on March, 12.

Magazines, newspapers and other sources:

General Anzeiger Bonn (2013 January 26): *Das Netzwerk der Gotteskrieger*. Retrieved from: www.general-anzeiger-bonn.de/bonn/themen/pronrw/Das-Netzwerk-der-Gotteskrieger-article956703.html on January 28, 2013.

NYPD (2007): *Radicalization in The West. The Homegrown Threat*. New York: New York Police Department. Retrieved from: http://www.nyc.gov/html/nypd/downloads/ pdf/public_information/NYPD_Report-Radicalization_in_the_West.pdf on March 22, 2013.

Rp-online.de (2013 January 10): *Zahl der Salafisten in NRW hat sich verdoppel"*. Retrieved from: http://www.rp-online.de/panorama/deutschland/zahl-der-salafisten-in-nrw-hat-sich-verdoppelt-1.3130150 on January 23, 2013.

UN Security Council 6765th meeting (May 4, 2012): *Security Council, Highlighting Changing Nature, Character of Scourge of Terrorism*. Retrieved from: https://www.un.org/News/Press/docs/2012/sc10636.doc.htm on April 22, 2013.

US Departement of Homeland Security (2010 December 5): *Terrorist Use of Social Networking. Facebook Case Study*. Retrieved from: http://publicintelligence.net/ufouoles-dhs-terrorist-use-of-social-networking-facebook-case-study/?utm_source=twitterfeed&utm_medium=twitter on April 2, 2013.

Jihadist websites and video portals:

www.attiyyah.wordpress.com/

www.Ansar1.info

www.izzahazzam.wordpress.com

www.attiyyah.wordpress.com/category/gimf/

www.ansarul-aseer.com

Groups on the social media platform Facebook:

Dawa Ffm (closed down by German authorities)

Die wahre Religion (Engl.: The true religion)

Salafi Dawah – authenthisches Wissen

Deutschlandistan

Independent Journalists

Ansarul Anseer

Die Stimme der Ummah (Engl.: The voice of the ummah)

Al-Risalah Medienpruduktion

Der Weg der Salaf (Engl.: The way of the Salafis)

Salafi Dawah – authentisches Wissen (Engl.: Salafi Dawah – authentic knwoledge)

Islamisches Erwachen (Engl.: Islamic awakening)

Salafimedia

Izzahazzam